Evil, Suffering, and God

Evil, Suffering, and God

Theological Soundings

OWEN F. CUMMINGS

CASCADE *Books* • Eugene, Oregon

EVIL, SUFFERING, AND GOD
Theological Soundings

Cascade Books
An Imprint of Wipf and Stock Publishers
199 W. 8th Ave., Suite 3
Eugene, OR 97401

www.wipfandstock.com

PAPERBACK ISBN: 979-8-3852-6267-0
HARDCOVER ISBN: 979-8-3852-6268-7
EBOOK ISBN: 979-8-3852-6269-4

Cataloguing-in-Publication data:

Names: Cummings, Owen F. [author].

Title: Evil, suffering, and God : theological soundings / by Owen F. Cummings.

Description: Eugene, OR: Cascade Books, 2026 | Includes bibliographical references.

Identifiers: ISBN 979-8-3852-6267-0 (paperback) | ISBN 979-8-3852-6268-7 (hardcover) | ISBN 979-8-3852-6269-4 (ebook)

Subjects: LCSH: Suffering—Religious aspects—Christianity. | Theodicy. | Good and evil. | Religion—Philosophy. | Suffering—Biblical teaching.

Classification: BT160 C866 2026 (paperback) | BT160 (ebook)

VERSION NUMBER 042426

Dedicated to
Cathy
mulier fortis

Contents

Introduction

Everything lives, moves, and has its being in God. Everything is grace, everything gift. The world is not random chaos but good. God is not nowhere but everywhere. This may be a hard teaching in times of pain, but the alternative is far worse.

—Janet M. Soskice[1]

The liturgy does not provide easy solutions to evil, but if we are open to it, faithful worship can teach us how to be present with the afflicted and share God's love with them.

—Rowan Crews[2]

In my early years as a teacher of theology I had the good fortune to be a member of a small study group in Birmingham, England, called "The Open End." The membership was quite mixed and included biblical scholars, patristic scholars, one Anglican bishop, and various philosophers of religion and theologians. In the latter group, two theologians in particular had made significant contributions to our thinking about the problem of evil and suffering in the Christian understanding. These were John H. Hick and Kenneth Surin.

1. Soskice, "Why *Creatio ex Nihilo* For Theology Today?," 52.

2. Crews, *Good Lord, Deliver Us*, 15.

Two other members of the Open End group, Daniel W. Hardy and David F. Ford, were systematic theologians collaborating together on a book that came out as *Jubilate: Theology in Praise*. Santiago Sia, the Filipino-Irish philosopher of religion, was not a member of the group but at the time was readying the publication of his monograph on the American process thinker Charles Hartshorne, with a particular interest in theodicy. It was exciting to be in the midst of these thinkers and ideas—evil and suffering within different philosophical contexts on the one hand and doxology or praise of God on the other.

I remain in their midst as it were, these two poles of critical analysis and doxology, and some fifty years or so later I am no less excited. That is the originating context of this book.

Chapter 1, "Believing in God," is the foundation of all that follows. It's not concerned with believing in God in some kind of general theistic fashion, but rather its concern is the trinitarian-christological God of traditional Christianity. This stands in stark contrast with a version of God that is above and beyond creation, an uninvolved God. The chapter has its subtitle: "Or, from One Herbert to Another!" The first Herbert is the early seventeenth-century priest-poet George Herbert, the second being the twentieth-century Thomist theologian Herbert McCabe, OP. Together, they present us with a fine approach to understanding God as Love, as in 1 John 4:16.

Chapter 2 takes us to "Theodicies and Their Limits." The chapter examines various philosophical approaches to reconciling God with the experience of evil and suffering. While these approaches can be helpful, none of them succeeds, the lack of success having to do largely with a non-trinitarian-christological perspective. This brief analysis and critique is followed up in chapter 3, "Thinking About Divine Omnipotence," a view of God as the omnipotent manager of all that is qualified, using especially some ideas of the late Augustinian theologian Tarcisius van Bavel. He is chosen as guide because of his clarity and simultaneously because of his grasp of the Christian tradition. Again, the direction is to move away from a distant God to a very involved God, the God who becomes incarnate.

The involvement of God is mapped first in chapters 4 and 5, gaining insight from the Scriptures of the Old Testament. They present no uniform point of view on evil and suffering, ranging rather from the "law of retribution" through a certain skepticism in Qoheleth, a move towards what I would describe as a "mystical turn." I recognize this mystical turn beginning with the Book of Job and ultimately leading us on to chapter 6, focusing on the mystical vision of the cross of Christ. The mystical turn found in Job lays the foundations for a trajectory that climaxes in St. Paul's work and that continues to inform the Christian tradition. At least it did, until the period of history and thought known as the Enlightenment. This is when I see a movement away from the traditional trinitarian-christological vision, a necessarily corporate vision with Christian self-understanding as the body of Christ, towards a radical individualism and a remote or uninvolved God.

Sometimes when people are facing great physical suffering they pray and hope for a miracle. Thus, chapter 7 examines the role of miracles. Miracles will be seen as more complex than they are popularly thought to be. To demonstrate this complexity, a range of contemporary thinkers will be engaged. The purpose is to assist ordinary Christians to move towards a more adult, more informed point of view.

Chapter 8 examines moral evil, the surd we call sin. The examination proceeds through two novelists: Graham Greene and William Styron. Their characters are fictional, of course, but are also arguably insights into our human fragility and weakness, the situation of everyone. I turn in chapter 9 to some contemporaries whose exemplary witness, much like the lives of the saints, provides us with encouragement and hope in the midst of great suffering, physical and mental. Finally, chapter 10, "Death and God's Lovely Presence," takes us to literally "the last things." A precis of eschatology will be outlined that correlates with the traditional understanding of God as Love.

This little book is not a systematic treatise on evil, suffering, and God. What it hopes to achieve is to offer Christians today an approach that really helps, that helps us all to remain beacons of hope and sacraments of love, even in the midst of great difficulties and trying circumstances.

There are so many people to thank, but first and foremost Cathy, spouse and lifetime companion, and Susan, our daughter, for all her hard work on the manuscript. Exchanges with Paul D. Murray of the University of Durham have been especially helpful. Matthew Wimer and Robin Parry of Cascade Books have been a constant source of encouragement and support bringing this little book to birth. My thanks to all.

1

Believing in God

Or, from One Herbert to Another!

The Christian notion is that God—ultimate reality—is nothing other than love.

—Robert Barron[1]

At the heart of the desperate suffering there is in the world, suffering we can do nothing to resolve or remove for good, there is an indestructible energy making for love. If we have grasped what Jesus is about, we can trust that this is what lies at the foundation of everything.

—Rowan D. Williams[2]

INTRODUCTION

Sooner or later, I believe, everyone needs to make a decision about life. Is life simply the span of time that each of us has followed by

1. Barron, "God," 268.
2. Williams, *Tokens of Trust*, 10.

nothing? Or, is life understood to be more than the span of our years? Is there some intelligibility to be had beyond the immediacy of the present day, a sense of "something" or perhaps "Someone" beyond? Ultimately, we have to choose. To choose not to choose is itself a choice. The choice that lies behind this little book is that there is, to put it minimally, "Someone" behind it all, for Christians the triune God.

Every book has a necessary beginning, something(s) presupposed. The fundamental presupposition of this book is the reality of God as God is understood in the Christian tradition. Central to this understanding is the conviction that if you think you have understood God, it is not God who has been understood. One never gets to the point where one can say with complete conviction, "Now I've got it! Now I have a comprehensive understanding of God." The fourth-century Cappadocian theologian, St. Gregory of Nyssa, coined a word for this unending search to understand God. He called it *epektasis*, which we might paraphrase as constant "straining forward on the upward climb that never stops."[3] One never reaches a final point of understanding. This has been a leitmotif in the history of Christian reflection on God. It is found both East and West, in the Scriptures, in patristic and in medieval theology, in the theology that has emerged in and after the sixteenth century, and in contemporary theology. Despite this traditional emphasis, it would be true to say that a large number of people do not feel the need to strain forward on the upward climb towards an understanding of God. Too often there is a contentment to rest passively with an understanding that is nothing short of mediocre. "Many people who would not dream of relying on the understanding of literature or the sciences they acquired as children are content to leave their juvenile theological convictions largely unexamined."[4] These are the words of the spiritual writer Kathleen Norris. They ring true. They ring true not just of people in general, as it were, but also of people who have had the opportunity and privilege of years of higher education. Sometimes when

3. Young, *Brokenness and Blessing*, 20.

4. Norris, *Acedia and Me*, 114.

such educated persons turn their hand to the critique of religion, the understanding of God and of the things of God that they entertain is juvenile indeed.

This is the case, for example, of Richard Dawkins the scientist, whose book *The God Delusion* received massive public exposure and acclaim. In his sustained attack on religion and especially on Christianity he reveals himself as holding what can only be called "juvenile theological convictions." There is no felt need in Dawkins for *epektasis* of any kind. He certainly has not informed himself of the multiple studies in theology, and indeed interdisciplinary studies, that go far beyond juvenile convictions about God and religion. The literary critic Terry Eagleton writes that Dawkins on theology is like "someone holding forth on biology whose only knowledge of the subject is the *British Book of Birds*."[5] The theologian Nicholas Lash comments that "one cannot imagine a physicist holding an atomic particle, or a zoologist a yak, with the same sustained contempt and loathing, the same cavalier disregard for accurate description, the same ignorance of the literature, with which Dawkins treats all religious beliefs, ideas and practices."[6] Dawkins maintains that he is attacking not just any particular version of God or gods, but all gods or God, however they are understood.[7] However, his own particular version of God or gods bears little or no resemblance to the understanding of reflective believers.

What exactly do we mean by "God"? How do we reconcile what we know to be "true" from our culture with our convictions about "God"? It seems to me that both questions are fundamentally important. The first one invites an understanding of God that is congruent with the received tradition of Christianity. The second one forces us to relate that to our actual and living circumstances today. This means that there is correlation of a kind between the two questions, and it will not do to attempt an answer to one but not the other.

5. Eagleton, "Lunging, Flailing, Mispunching."
6. Lash, *Theology for Pilgrims*, 4.
7. Dawkins, *God Delusion*, 36.

Ideas of God that flow from reflection on certain human experiences point to the reality of God but without grasping or comprehending the reality. Since all human language necessarily structures and expresses our experience and understanding of the things of the world, what we might call creation, when language is applied to God, who is not a thing of the world, not creation, that language can be applied only in a metaphorical or analogous way. Herbert McCabe, the twentieth-century Thomist theologian whom we shall meet later in this chapter had a neat way of expressing this conviction when he said that all language for God is "second-hand clothing": "We always do have to speak of our God with borrowed words; it is one of the special things about our God that there are no peculiarly appropriate words that belong to him. . . . He is always dressed verbally in second-hand clothes that don't fit him very well. We always have to be on guard against taking these clothes as revealing who and what he is."[8] Second-hand clothing is not made-to-measure but is ill-fitting, and yet it sort of does what needs to be done. All language for God is like that. It does not fit, it cannot fit the reality of God, but it sort of does what needs to be done to avoid saying nothing at all. Language for God must be understood metaphorically, not literally.

Metaphors for God are drawn both impersonally and personally. For example, impersonal metaphors include "a mighty Fortress," "light," "a rock of refuge," and so forth. Personal metaphors include father, mother, husband, king, lord, and so forth. Given the patriarchal culture that produced the Hebrew Scriptures and the New Testament, it is hardly surprising that the majority of personal metaphors are masculine rather than feminine. While that is understandable, it becomes problematic "if male figures predominate to such an extent that God somehow appears to be more appropriately represented as male rather than female."[9] While we have no access to God other than through images, no image is ever entirely adequate and every image will always represents to some extent a distortion. There is no way to the reality

8. McCabe, *God Still Matters*, 3.

9. Wright, "God," 426.

of God except through the image we have of God, and that image is always to some extent a distortion. This is why the *Catechism of the Catholic Church*, for example, insists upon purifying images of God: "We must continually purify our language of everything in it that is limited, image-bound or imperfect, if we are not to confuse our image of God—'the inexpressible, the incomprehensible, the invisible, the ungraspable'—with our human representations. Our human words always fall short of the mystery of God."[10] While we may, as the *Catechism* encourages, constantly purify our images of God, it is extremely difficult to see how we can quite get beyond these images. There simply is no other way to think of and to speak about God, and, indeed, to pray to God. At the same time, if our faith is to mature, there needs to be some element of critical reflection about God, even if paradoxically we can never reach an understanding that is absolutely satisfactory.

One such critical reflection is provided by John H. Wright. He proposed a three-step pattern that may be discerned in divine and human interaction. The first step is God taking the absolute initiative. This is God creating out of pure love and gratuitousness, the reason there is something rather than nothing. This is God's grace at work and is antecedent to any response. The second step is the response of the human creature to this initiative of God. Whenever a human being acts freely, she or he is aligning self with God, or is departing in some measure from God. It should be pointed out that this response of the human creature to God may, in fact, be anonymous in respect of God. God is always known but not always named and recognized. The third step is God responding to the creature's response to the divine initiative. God is affected by the action of his creatures. Wright points out that these three steps should not be thought of simply in terms of chronological succession, though time is obviously involved. The steps represent an analytic interpretation of divine–human interaction. "The future does set before us the initiative of God's love and the past embodies the divine judgment, but at all times in the present, God is here in gracious love, inclining and illuminating the created agent, and

10. *Catechism of the Catholic Church*, no. 42.

the free creature is more or less accepting the gracious love of God (or refusing it), and God is responding in effective judgment. In this way God is profoundly immanent in our lives and in the whole course of human and cosmic history, guiding events and accomplishing his gracious purpose."[11]

DISTORTED WAYS OF THINKING ABOUT GOD

This reflective interpretation, however, is not the way everyone thinks, and is not the way everyone images God. Here is what I mean. In 1949, before his conversion, the American Trappist theologian Thomas Merton wrote the following words: "I never had an adequate notion of what Christians meant by God. I had simply taken for granted that the God in whom religious people believed and to whom they attributed the creation and government of all things was a noisy and dramatic and passionate character, a vague, jealous, hidden being, the objectification of all their own subjective ideals."[12] One suspects that many contemporaries would share views like this. Such views have passed into our culture from the world of psychology and ultimately from the world of philosophy through the thought, for example, of Ludwig Feuerbach. God, he believed, is simply a projection of our own subjective ideals and needs.

What are some of these common distorted images of God? Pulling examples from different authors and sources we might compile the following list. First, God as cosmic moralist. Behind this image lies the idea that since God is the divine lawgiver and judge, he keeps careful records of all human offenses and ultimately will punish offenders. Needless to say, there is a far more positive association of God with morality than this, but it is a fairly common distorted image. Second, God as controlling power. This image understands God as determining every detail of the world. Not just the large details, as it were, such as a tsunami, or

11. Wright, "God," 434.

12. Merton, *Elected Silence*, 138–39.

an earthquake, or other such natural phenomena, but the small details too, such as God's choosing to "take" a particular life at a particular time. Undoubtedly, the various Christian traditions have nuanced and sophisticated ways of thinking about God's power, but at the popular level this notion of God as controlling power is widespread. Third, God as sanctioner of the *status quo*. This is the God understood as the protector and custodian of the way things are. The present order is provided by God and protected by God. It is divinely willed and to challenge it is to challenge God. Here again one may find sophisticated versions of this image, but crudely presented, it is simply unacceptable. The reason is that the *status quo* too often is disinterested in the promotion of a more just and equitable social and political order. A God who was the custodian of an unjust social order, however defended by the pundits, would be no God at all in the Christian sense. Fourth, God as male. At least in Christianity there is a very long-standing tradition of thinking about God in masculine terms, as already noted. Obviously, Jesus of Nazareth was a man. However, the other two persons of the Trinity are also thought of in male terms: God the "Father" obviously so, and the Holy Spirit is often spoken of as "he." Many thoughtful Christian thinkers no longer find this a helpful way of talking about God. Alternative ways of speaking about God and to God have not met with universal acceptance at this point.[13] A greater degree of tolerance among Christians is required here. There is no room for an unreflective or positivist dogmatism that in principle disallows any change from scriptural ways of speaking about God.

FINDING OTHER WAYS

Arguably, the most precious experience and value that human beings have is love. It hardly needs to be pointed out that "love" has been rendered banal, superficial, and cheap in so many different ways in our culture. Love is best understood as a process

13. The interested reader might wish to look at some of David Ford's careful thoughts in *Shape of Living*, 181–84.

of self-donation to another person. Calling love a process moves us away from seeing it simplistically as one experience or as one action. It is much better thought of as a sequence of experiences or actions. Describing love as self-donation means that love is about literally giving oneself to another. This giving may take a variety of expressions. Each expression, however, is intended symbolically to stand for one's entire self. In saying authentically to someone "I love you," one is intentionally saying to the other, "All that I am and all that I have is for you."

In the first letter of St. John this is how God is described: "God is love, and those who abide in love abide in God, and God abides in them" (1 John 4:16). In so far as it is possible to speak of an essence of Christianity, it seems to me to be this: that God is Love, that God is the unbounded, unconditional, eternal Process of Self-Donation. "Love" is God's best name, we might say. Thus, to say "God is" is to say "God loves." Probably many Christians would ally themselves with this way of thinking. To interiorize this conviction is difficult and takes time, a lifetime. The theologian James T. Burtchaell has it right when he says, "There is nothing very astonishing about a God who loves us relentlessly, except that we generally do not believe in one."[14] It is not particularly astonishing to claim that God loves humankind relentlessly. The claim is based, as we have seen, both in human experience and in the text of the New Testament. What happens, however, is that experiences and false understandings and interpretations, inculcated over perhaps a long period of time, get in the way of appropriating the deep meaning of this claim. The way a person is brought up, the way in which she or he is educated and nurtured, life experiences, all affect how one thinks of and how one images God.

This book is written from the fundamental axiom of belief in God. What does it mean to believe in God? The question seems simple and clear enough, but it is really very complex. For a start, we need to have some basic content for the word "God," that is, we need to learn the meaning of the word. "We have to learn the meanings of the words we use, and it is the same with the word

14. Burtchaell, *Philemon's Problem*, 41.

'god.'"[15] We get those meanings initially from the significant people who form and nurture us—parents and guardians, pastors and teachers, peers and companions. As we move through life, the sheer experience of life allied to our innate quest to understand will refine and expand in various ways this initial content for the word "God."

We might say, therefore, that there are two necessary constitutive elements we bring to understanding of the word "God": culture and experience. Culture stands for the tradition into which we are born, and experience is the particular determination and response to culture that each person is. There is a reciprocity between culture and experience. As I am shaped and molded by a culture/tradition, I shape and mold that culture/tradition through my own personal pattern of experience.

This is an abstract way of speaking. Let's speak more concretely by focusing on two Herberts! First, the culture and experience of George Herbert (1593–1633), the Anglican priest-poet, and second, the culture and experience of the Catholic theologian Herbert McCabe, OP (1926–2001).

GEORGE HERBERT (1593–1633)

"One of the gifts of God to Anglicans, and through them to the whole Church, is the poetry and prose of George Herbert."[16] There is a legion of excellent books and one periodical, *The George Herbert Journal*, on the poetry of George Herbert, from both a literary and theological point of view. Though I have read deeply in this secondary Herbert literature, my intention here is spiritual and theological. It is an invitation to enter the spiritual and theological world of Herbert's words so that in encounter with these words we may be gifted and challenged, transformed and cleansed.

Why George Herbert? Certainly, Herbert is one of the finest English poets, with outstanding poetic skill, but that is not my

15. Ford, *Theology*, 35.

16. Sykes, *Unashamed Anglicanism*, 49.

major reason for choosing him. Again, Herbert's Anglicanism invites a Catholic like me to extend his horizons to be enriched by an ecclesial tradition other than his own. That is a fine and worthy goal, but that, too, is not my primary reason. I have chosen George Herbert because my head and heart are full of George Herbert, and I find his theological ideas, images, and thoughts attractive, inspiring, and most helpful.

Donald Allchin, commenting on our human penchant for visiting the places associated with our heroes, says of George Herbert, "It is one thing to know that George Herbert gave up a promising career in Cambridge and London in order to bury himself in an insignificant country parish. It is another to kneel before the altar in the tiny church at Bemerton."[17] The Bemerton church is where George Herbert served as a priest, and where he is buried. Kneeling before the altar in Bemerton might lead one to recognize not only something of Herbert's sanctity and commitment, but equally that we are all, as Christians, drawn to the service of the *communio*. While few may be able to kneel before the altar in Bemerton, all can feel the pull of God's presence and service in engaging Herbert's thoughts. We may kneel before the Lord anywhere with Herbert's words and poetry.

There has been much debate about the roots of Herbert's theology. Stephen Sykes writes, "Perhaps . . . we should be readier to say simply that Herbert was an Anglican."[18] Some commentators stress his medieval background, while others give emphasis to his Reformation ancestry. Of course, behind the Reformation authors lie the theological giants of the patristic and medieval periods, to whom they necessarily react whether positively or negatively. These are the authors who were the "texts" of the sixteenth century. Herbert tells us himself in *A Priest to the Temple* (1632) that "the country Parson hath read the Fathers also, and the Schoolmen, and the later writers, or a good proportion of all." Given his times, it is inconceivable that Herbert would not have read among the

17. Allchin, *World Is a Wedding*, 148.

18. Sykes, *Unashamed Anglicanism*, 49.

"later writers" some of the Reformers.[19] There are times when one will find anti-Catholic sentiment in some of his poems, the unfortunate and mutual polemic of the times between Catholic and Reformed. When the church is split by human sinfulness, no one can be entirely free of the infection.

"To many people Herbert is an uncanonized saint, perhaps a mystic."[20] He has had a profound influence on many people, not only in the past but also in our own times. Ralph Vaughan Williams, for example, set some of his poems to music in his justly famous *Five Mystical Songs*. The French religious thinker Simone Weil (1909–43) also came under his influence, especially the poem "Love III." Distrustful of more conventional expressions of piety and devotion, Weil had what can only be called a mystical experience of God's presence, and associated it with Herbert's poem, "Love III."[21] Weil wrote, "I enclose the English poem, Love, which I recited to you. It has played a big role in my life." Many have felt drawn to a profound sense of God's presence through reading Herbert. However, I have chosen to engage not "Love III" but an earlier poem, "Discipline."

Throw away thy rod,
Throw away thy wrath:
    O my God,
Take the gentle path.

For my heart's desire
Unto thine is bent:
    I aspire
To a full consent.

Not a word or look
I affect to own,
    But by book,
And thy book alone.

Though I fail, I weep:

19. Sykes, *Unashamed Anglicanism*, 49.

20. Sheldrake, *Love Took My Hand*, 2.

21. See the introduction by Leslie Fiedler in Weil, *Waiting for God*, xxii–xxiii.

Though I halt in pace,
  Yet I creep
To the throne of grace.

Then let wrath remove;
Love will do the deed:
  For with love
Stony hearts will bleed.

Love is swift of foot;
Love's a man of war,
  And can shoot,
And can hit from far.

Who can 'scape his bow?
That which wrought on thee,
  Brought thee low,
Needs must work on me.

Throw away thy rod;
Though man frailties hath,
  Thou art God:
Throw away thy wrath.

Immediately we can see that the poem is addressed to "God." It is a prayer. Herbert asks God to throw away his wrath in the first and last stanzas. God for him has been associated with wrath, with anger. "Rod" seems to have a punitive meaning, as in "spare the rod and spoil the child," even if the punishment is ultimately for the good of the one struck. Herbert asks God to throw away everything that smacks of punishment and anger, and he asks God to "Take the gentle path." This request, however, is prefaced by the words, "O *my* God." In addressing God as "my God," Herbert moves into deep, personal expression—"Take the gentle path with me."

In the second stanza the poet speaks of the basis of this personal expression. He tells God that the desire of his heart is to be in complete concord with God. God's word, God's book, Holy Scripture, is to be the foundation of his life, according to stanza three. Stanza four shows us Herbert weeping at his failures yet continuing to creep slowly toward this God of grace. The first line of stanza five recapitulates the thrust of the first and final stanzas, "Then let wrath remove." Wrath has no place with God because God is Love—"Love will do the deed." Love, not anger, has the power to make living hearts out of stony hearts, thinking of Ezekiel 36:26: "A new heart I will give you, and a new spirit I will put within you; and I will remove from your body the heart of stone and give you a heart of flesh." Petrified hearts melt before and are metamorphosed by Love.

The next two stanzas tell us that this Divine Love is an excellent warrior and bowman. None can escape his loving aim, this loving aim that now "must work on [Herbert]." Stanza eight acknowledges our human frailty, but God is not wrathful. He is Love. Notice the very strong language of stanza seven. Herbert is continuing to address God. God as Love was "brought low"—that is to say, made human—in the incarnation of the Eternal Word. The motive for the incarnation is God's very nature as Love, in a sense constraining God to share human life and experience—"that which wrought on thee." Now this same Love, God reaching out, divine grace, must work on Herbert to transform him.

HERBERT MCCABE, OP (1926–2001)

There are many different ways of thinking about God. In a very useful book published in 1971, the Reformed theologian Huw Parri Owen (1926–96) set out and critiqued ten concepts of God that differed from his own brand of "classical theism."[22] Owen was in many ways a traditional Christian who espoused the traditional classical way of thinking about God, which developed from the early centuries of Christianity but gained its classical understanding in the Middle Ages, not least in the philosophical theology of St. Thomas Aquinas. While Owen's work is a good road map for thinking about God, in my judgment it does not come close to the expression of Herbert McCabe, the Dominican philosopher-theologian.

22. Owen, *Concepts of Deity*.

Herbert McCabe, OP, was one of the finest English-language Thomists of the twentieth century. His profound engagement with the work of St. Thomas Aquinas, in alliance with contemporary philosophy and theology, and his crisp prose enabled him to reach many who would never have read a page of Aquinas. Let us turn to some of McCabe's thinking about God through a series of points:

- "Aquinas' Five Ways are sketches for five arguments to show that a certain kind of question about our world and ourselves is valid: 'Why the world, instead of nothing at all?'"[23] The Five Ways of Aquinas are understood here to be provocative ways of responding to the question why does anything exist.
- "The creator cannot be outside his creature. . . . If the creator is the reason for everything that is, there can be no actual being which does not have the creator as its center holding it in being."[24] Here is no spectator God, reigning in splendor above creation, but rather a deeply involved creator, nowhere absent.
- "At the heart of every creature is the source of *esse*, making it to be and to act (ST, 1a, 8, 1, c)."[25] "The creative causal power of God does not operate on me from outside, as an alternative to me; it is the creative causal power of God that makes me *me*."[26] This is in its own way a stunning observation. Not only is God not a spectator observing me from afar, but God is closer to me than I am to myself. "We are not objects of the Godhead, but by being in Christ, we are within the Godhead."[27]
- "We always do have to speak of our God with borrowed words; it is one of the special things about our God that there are no peculiarly appropriate words that belong to him. . . .

23. McCabe, "Involvement of God," 40.
24. McCabe, "Involvement of God," 44–45.
25. McCabe, "Involvement of God," 46.
26. McCabe, "Involvement of God," xiii.
27. McCabe, *God Still Matters*, 8.

> He is always dressed verbally in second-hand clothes that don't fit him very well. We always have to be on guard against taking these clothes as revealing who and what he is."[28] No words are fully adequate to the reality of God. This, I believe, is McCabe's folksy approach to the traditional doctrine of analogy.

This is the God with whom we have to do in this attempt to understand something about evil and suffering in human life. No other God will do.

28. McCabe, *God Still Matters*, 3.

2

Theodicies and Their Limits

There are no unproblematic solutions to evil—it is even questionable whether it is right to see it in terms of a problem with some conceivable intellectual solution. Is an attempt to solve it not to trivialize it? Surely it is above all a practical problem which calls for practical responses? Yet most practical responses require thought and intelligence, and stopping thinking about evil is no solution either.

—David F. Ford[1]

How does the good creation of God come to be so marred with evil? We will never have a complete answer to such a question. But the religious tradition, going back to biblical times, has seen at least part of the answer to lie in the reality of human freedom and the destructive exercise of that human power. This is what lies at the heart of the doctrine of sin.

—Zachary Hayes[2]

1. Ford, *Theology*, 73.
2. Hayes, *Gift of Being*, 87.

INTRODUCTION

Some years ago I was leading an in-service theology course for the priests of a diocese. One of the concerns was thinking about love, especially the idea that "God is Love" (1 John 4:16). Some time had been spent trying to unpack what this meant when a priest raised his hand, asking, "How is it possible to speak of God as Love to someone who is in terrible circumstances, perhaps someone who is dying?" What a wonderfully difficult question! By way of my halting response I suggested that the most we can do as pastoral ministers in such dire contexts is to console, especially through the sacraments, to encourage hope and trust in God. However, it is surely much better to cultivate regularly a hopeful and trusting Christian spirituality long before the troubling trials and tribulations of life come our way. The reflections in this book attempt to do just that, to cultivate a hopeful and trusting spirituality through careful thinking and praying, using the many rich traditions that have come down to us.

SUFFERING AND THEODICY

The existential meaning of suffering is obvious to all human beings, but it may be helpful to see it described.

> Suffering may be defined as any experience that impinges on an individual's or a community's sense of well-being. Synonyms include pain, grief, distress, disruption, affliction, imposition, oppression, discrimination, and any sense of loss or of being victimized. The negative experience may be physical, psychological, interpersonal, or spiritual, though in most instances it involves a combination of these. Suffering, then, is one's consciousness of life's dark side, the human experience that all is not peaceful and harmonious in our bodies, in our souls, in our relationships, and the cosmos.[3]

3. Sparks, "Suffering," 950.

That is a very comprehensive description of human suffering and most of us will be able to see in it expressions to which we can relate quite easily.

Suffering is linked inevitably to the problem of evil, often known by the technical term theodicy. The word "theodicy," first coined seemingly by the philosopher G. W. Leibniz in 1710, comes from two Greek roots: *Theos*, meaning God; and *dike* meaning justice. Taken together as "theodicy," the word means justifying or defending the goodness of God against objections arising from the experience of evil and suffering. Theodicy became a more widespread philosophical concern with the onset of the seventeenth- and eighteenth-century movement known as the Enlightenment.[4] There were various reasons for this more recent Enlightenment concern with theodicy. For a start, many thinkers were simply scandalized by the many European wars of religion that followed upon the Protestant Reformation of the sixteenth century, most often involving the slaughter of religious opponents. As a result, many philosophically inclined people found wanting the practices and dogmas of particular churches that pitted Protestants and Catholics against each other, and this led to a flight from traditional authorities. Evil and suffering had always been a challenge for thoughtful Christians down through the ages, but now, because the Christian tradition of doctrine and dogma—including doctrines of the Trinity, of Christ, of the church, and of the sacraments—were being called into question, solutions or responses to the challenge were being sought *outside of* that trinitarian-christological doctrinal synthesis.[5]

Many discussions of the theodicy question became filtered through an understanding of "God" that is constrained by the Enlightenment principles of philosophical theism, distant in many respects from the approach to God outlined in the first chapter. Without the traditional trinitarian-christological-ecclesial-sacramental axis, rooted in the God who is nothing but Love, "the divinity of modern theism thus turns out to be '*a*' being (an implicit

4. See Tilley, *Evils of Theodicy*, 221.

5. See Kilby, *God, Evil and the Limits of Theology*, 67–84.

stress is invariably placed on the indefinite article), a rare and fascinating 'entity', possessing a number of clearly specifiable characteristics. Theism is then simply to be understood as a hypothesis about this most sublime 'entity.'"[6] God has become an entity, albeit the supreme entity. Kenneth Surin continues in this vein:

> These discussions, then, assume that "God" is a unipersonal being, certainly not the God of traditional Trinitarian Christianity, and furthermore, that this "God" is intelligible. . . . To think that God can be understood as some kind of "thing" or "entity," one could say, is to have the most profound misunderstanding of who God is. It is to leave theological utterance in irreparable disarray.[7]

Given that we can never finally comprehend God, that God is the sheer inexhaustible Mystery that is Love and not another entity, even the greatest one, is there any point in proceeding with the enterprise of theodicy? Is there any point in reaching towards a theoretical answer to the challenges that evil and suffering pose?

I think there is a point in searching for an answer. At the very least, such searching and probing may help us discard answers that seem unworthy of the Christian God as that God is revealed in Scripture, Christian tradition, and in the light of our own reflected personal experience of evil and suffering. Tarcisius van Bavel writes,

> Are theoretical answers really meaningful in such a situation? I believe they are, because they can provide direction for our attempts to come to terms with suffering, and they prevent us from aggravating our suffering by interpreting it in an improper fashion—though it remains the case that no theoretical answer can spare us the task of coping personally with the suffering that touches our lives.[8]

6. Surin, *Theology and the Problem of Evil*, 5.
7. Surin, *Theology and the Problem of Evil*, 7.
8. Van Bavel, "Meaninglessness of Suffering," 129.

Looking at what theologians and philosophers of religion have to say, and acknowledging the risk of over simplification, we can group their reflections into four basic categories:

- evil as the privation of good
- explaining evil by trying to demonstrate what purposes it might serve
- process approaches to theodicy
- "action" approaches to theodicy

EVIL AS THE PRIVATION OF GOOD

Privative theodicies, associated with St. Augustine, St. Thomas Aquinas, and most Catholic theologians, claim that evil is not something in itself but is the absence or the privation of good. It finds its inspiration in the creation stories of the book of Genesis. God creates everything good, but evil enters into the world when humans sin, turning away from God. For Aquinas and Augustine, evil is a privation of good because God creates *ex nihilo*/out of nothing, and if evil were a thing, a being, the conclusion would have to be that God created evil directly. Evil is not willed by God. God merely permits free agents to do evil and to suffer evil. Augustine's theology shifts the problem of evil to the sphere of human willing; his vision is exclusively moral. Leaving aside the issue of physical evil, seeing suffering as punishment for sin—individual or collective, known or unknown—is problematic. It is problematic not least because "this penal vision shatters against a wall of disproportionate and innocent suffering."[9]

9. Duffy, "Evil," 362.

EXPLAINING EVIL BY SHOWING WHAT PURPOSES IT SERVES IN OUR WORLD

The world is in the process of becoming, so that creation is an unfinished project. Evil and suffering are to be understood as "the natural spin-off, the inevitable growing pains of matter and spirit evolving from fetal immaturity into the fullness of being."[10] That means that the realities of pain and suffering, as well as those of temptation and sin, are necessary for human beings to develop ultimately into people worthy to share life in communion with God. One theologian has called this approach the "educative instrumentality of natural evil."[11]

A key classic example here is the very fine work of John Hick (1922–2012), *Evil and the God of Love* (1966), and, at the level of popular apologetics, C. S. Lewis (1898–1963). Hick refers to his hypothesis of "soul-making," and it has been well described as follows:

> Temptation, sin, and suffering are necessary conditions if egoistic humans are to become loving persons worthy of life with God. History is person-making pedagogy in which the world's rough edges and painful growth are needed if people are to develop virtue and freely turn to a hidden, uncoercive God out of love, not compulsion. God could eliminate evil, but at the price of creating unheroic humanity, a race of pampered children. God is powerful enough to spoil humans, but too wise and good to do so.[12]

Hick has been credited with developing the contrast between two different theodicies, the Augustinian and the Irenaean, after Saints Augustine (354–430) and Irenaeus (c. 130–c. 202), the former representing the Latin/Western tradition and the latter the Greek/Eastern tradition. For the Augustinian (and Thomist) approach, God created a perfect world from which humans fell,

10. Sparks, "Suffering," 951.

11. Macquarrie, *Principles of Christian Theology*, 258.

12. Duffy, "Evil," 362.

per the Genesis creation narratives. In the Irenaean approach, God created a world that was not perfect, but rather a world designed for human beings to develop and grow in spiritual perfection. Irenaeus distinguishes between the "image" (*eikon*) of God and the "likeness" (*homoiosis*) of God in humankind. The challenge is for humans to grow from the image into the likeness. Our less than perfect world is the environment designed to enable that growth.

C. S. Lewis wrote two books in which is set out his theodicy: *The Problem of Pain* (1949) and *A Grief Observed* (1963). For Lewis pain is "God's megaphone," which God uses to wake us up from our inadequate faith and bring us to a more mature form of faith.[13] Pain and suffering are used by God to open us up to the reality of God's salvation and to spiritual health.

The problem with the point of view of Hick and Lewis, however, is that while suffering may indeed have the capacity to enable people to grow spiritually it can also absolutely crush those who suffer. In the words of theodicist Terrence Tilley,

> It is hard to see that there is any appreciable difference between such a God so thoroughly obscured by evil and no God at all. Moreover, they image God as a harsh schoolmaster, "educating" humans in the school of very hard knocks: could God not have found a better pedagogy than the Holocaust to educate people? For individuals, suffering does not always make a person better. All too often, suffering does not ennoble but diminishes and destroys a person.[14]

PROCESS THEODICY

Process theodicy, based on the thinking of philosophers Alfred North Whitehead and Charles Hartshorne, is different from these first two approaches. Process theodicy redefines key terms in the traditional approaches, for example, what is meant by divine

13. Lewis, *Problem of Pain*, 83.

14. Tilley, "Evil, Problem of," 361.

power or omnipotence. For process thinkers, divine power is redefined to be only the power of persuasion or attraction, and never of coercion. "Divine power is only the limited power of persuasion as God eternally attempts to lure the world's entities to their greatest individual and collective good. Evil is the cost of this evolution." Though, as Stephen Duffy points out, "Such a limited God's success seems dubious, given evil's saturation of the planet."[15]

However, for some Christian thinkers in this process stream of thought, matters are not just left at that, with evil and suffering as the price for evolutionary progress. Consider these words from a Catholic process theologian, Thomas E. Hosinski, commenting on God's responsibility for evil and suffering: "This is analogous to the way in which parents, by giving life to their children, are in a sense responsible for the fact that their children will inevitably suffer and die. Does it make any sense to blame parents for this? They can do nothing to change the fact that all living things suffer and die, and yet their love compels them to share the gift of life with their children. Analogously, God's love compels God to give the gift of life to the universe, despite the inevitability of suffering, tragedy and death. But unlike human parents God can overcome the limitations of finitude by taking all things into God's own unending life."[16] Hosinski's analogy, even with its obvious limitations, is attractive. The final clause—"taking all things into God's own unending life"—emancipates the analogy from anthropomorphism. While God may be likened to loving parents, he is so much more as he overcomes human limitations.

"ACTION" THEODICY

Thus far the theodicies we have been describing are intellectual, that is to say, an intellectual analysis is brought to bear on reconciling the reality of God with evil and suffering in the world. There

15. Duffy, "Evil," 363. See also Kilby, *God, Evil and the Limits of Theology*, who writes, "Process theology sacrifices the traditional picture of God to achieve an intelligible system that allows for evil."

16. Hosinski, *Image of the Unseen God*, 168.

is another approach to the issue, an approach that emphasizes action in the face of evil and suffering. Briefly, it is the approach that maintains, "In solidarity, people can enable each other to face evil of every kind without denying its reality. . . . Suffering is not abolished or explained but faced."[17]

Probably the best example of action theodicy comes from Rabbi Harold Kushner. Harold Kushner published *When Bad Things Happen to Good People* in 1981 and from the point of view of non-technical theology was immensely successful and influential. The book is very moving because it is the fruit of Rabbi Kushner's struggle with the premature death of his son after a prolonged illness. He argues that while God is limited in power, his goodness is not limited. For Kushner, evil "happens for no reason," and is the result of randomness and simply bad luck. His point of view is best summarized in his own words:

> I can worship a God who hates suffering but cannot eliminate it, more easily than I can worship a God who chooses to make children suffer and die. . . . Let me suggest that the bad things that happen to us in our lives do not have a meaning when they happen to us. They do not happen for any good reason which would cause us to accept them willingly. But we can give them a meaning. We can redeem these tragedies from senselessness by imposing meaning on them. The question we should be asking is not, "Why did this happen to me? What did I do to deserve this?" That is really an unanswerable, pointless question. A better question would be "Now that this has happened to me, what am I going to do about it?"[18]

Action theodicy is an approach to which many people can relate. Many decent, ordinary people want to help in a variety of ways when evil and suffering occur. They visit those who suffer to bring comfort and companionship. In times of bereavement, for example, many communities come together by preparing food for those who grieve. When natural disasters such as a tsunami occur,

17. Tilley, "Evil, Problem of," 362.

18. Kushner, *When Bad Things Happen to Good People*, 134–36.

countless numbers of people contribute financially to alleviate suffering.

THE FINAL CONTRIBUTION OF KARL RAHNER, SJ (1904–84)

Karl Rahner was one of the most influential theologians of the twentieth century. Just a couple of weeks before he died he wrote a brief article, "Saying Yes to God with Hope and Love," for the British Catholic newspaper *The Universe*. In fact, this was the last article written by Rahner before his death. The central part of his contribution is this: Suffering is incomprehensible. The incomprehensibility of suffering is part of the incomprehensibility of God. Neither may be grasped by the human intellect. "The finite mind must necessarily accept God as the incomprehensible One, believing with a firm hold and loving with a selfless love that this incomprehensibility is the only true fulfillment of our existence, . . . accepting God in hope and love as incomprehensible mystery."[19] There is something absolutely compelling about this point of view, but seeking an understanding of the faith, I believe, impels us to probe this incomprehensible mystery of evil and suffering, even as we adore the Mystery of God.

Let me make some brief comments on this admittedly all too brief synopsis of Rahner's position. First, I think Rahner is right. The incomprehensibility of evil/suffering and the incomprehensibility of God shade into one another. And yet we have an innate need to understand reality, an insatiable drive to understand. It is the source of science and technology, of advances in medical care for which, of course, we are all so grateful. This desire to understand is the energy that gives rise to all great literature, art, and music that go beyond the superficial level of instant entertainment. We want to know, we want to understand, we want to grasp reality. We can never abandon this innate desire to understand without lapsing into chaos, without life becoming just one darn thing after

19. Rahner, "Saying Yes to God."

another. In my very limited attempt to understand, either this life is just one darn thing after another, or it evokes thanksgiving and praise. Not withstanding the realities of evil and suffering, it seems to me that ultimately many of us are grateful for existence. We are glad to be. That gladness-to-be can flourish into gratitude, to thanksgiving. We want to say, "Thank you." Not only that, there is for many of us a desire to praise the Source of this existence that we call "God." This, for me, is the equivalent of Job 13:15 in the King James Version: "Even though he slay me, yet will I trust him."

3

Thinking About Divine Omnipotence

It is important to keep in mind from the very outset that theological thought about God is thought about a mystery. I mention this here because it influences an attitude to be adopted in the effort to talk about God. I mean an attitude of respect that is incompatible with the kind of God-talk that is sure, at times arrogantly sure, that it knows everything there is to know about God.

—Gustavo Gutiérrez[1]

Phoebe is the niece of Fr. John who has been invited to supper with his sister Kate and her family. The conversation turns to the problem of evil.

> *"Uncle John, do you think God really loves us—I mean, really, really loves us?" John's heart sinks. The question is asked with the utmost seriousness. . . . "Yes, of course I think God loves us," he says. "I told*

1. Gutiérrez, *On Job*, xi.

my Religious Education teacher you're a priest," says Phoebe. "She told me I should ask how you can believe in a good and powerful God when there's so much suffering in the world."

—Tina Beattie[2]

INTRODUCTION: JOHN COTTINGHAM AND CREATION

Christians profess in the traditional creeds the omnipotence of God: "I believe in God the Father almighty, maker of heaven and earth." God is hereby affirmed as both omnipotent and as creator. In the last half of the twentieth century there have been attempts to revisit the doctrine of creation and of what it means to affirm that God is omnipotent, both of which are increasingly complex issues.[3] Let's begin this chapter on divine omnipotence with some sage reflections of John Cottingham, philosopher of religion.[4]

First, Cottingham begins with an abstract philosophical possibility. Perhaps, he maintains, God should have confined his creation to an eternally bliss-filled world, a world in which no suffering of any kind ever occurred. However, while this as a metaphysical possibility must be admitted—what the philosophical theologian Richard Swinburne has called a "toy world"—"what God could not do . . . is put us in *this* world, the world of matter, and also simultaneously make our existence on this earth eternal and blissful."[5] If this world as God's creation is to be valued, it will necessarily be marked by stress, power, terror, grandeur, danger, as well as by incredible beauty and vividness.

So, secondly, we need to move away from a "managed" world to a God who "lets things be." "Divine creation, it seems, necessarily involves letting-go, allowing for the unfolding of the material

2. Beattie, *Good Priest*, 134.

3. For creation, see, for example, Cummings, *How Great Thou Art.*

4. Cottingham, *Spiritual Dimension*, 18–36.

5. Cottingham, *Spiritual Dimension*, 31.

world" as we now have it. Third, Cottingham briefly contemplates the alternative. "The impulse *not* to let go, not to withdraw but to hurry back in, is of course one that every parent knows, but it is also clear that any parent who wishes to allow a child independence, self-development, growth, and fulfillment, must vacate the space."[6] One might be given to think that while this analogy is compelling for limited human beings, it does not apply to the infinitude that is God. Not so, says Cottingham, at least not if this world is the world that God wants.

At the same time, we're not left with a deistic God, a God at a distance from his creation, a God who started things off but has now withdrawn. For the incarnation must be considered—the God who is Love has not only created this kind of world but has entered this world "not as a superior being, or as a fussy micro-manager, but on its own terms, utterly unprotected and vulnerable."[7] Finally, maintains Cottingham, this unprotected and utterly vulnerable God remains with us, and moreover, invites us to pass over into him in the Eucharist. The movement of God becomes the human movement.

TARCISIUS VON BAVEL ON DIVINE OMNIPOTENCE

Having introduced this chapter with the perspective of John Cottingham, let us now go on to reflect on the meaning of divine omnipotence by using the thought of theologian Tarcisius van Bavel (1923–2007). Tarcisius Jan van Bavel was a Catholic priest and Augustinian friar, and an internationally respected authority on the theology of St. Augustine. He was professor of systematic theology at the Catholic University of Leuven, Belgium. In a carefully worded essay entitled "Where Is God When Human Beings Suffer?," he discusses divine omnipotence.

6. Cottingham, *Spiritual Dimension*, 33.

7. Cottingham, *Spiritual Dimension*, 34.

Speaking of creation, Van Bavel writes, "[God] wishes to give existence to something outside himself, something possessed of a certain freedom and autonomy. His wish is for people who can choose him in freedom, since real love always involves a free choice. . . . That same freedom means, however, that the other may *not* choose me. It is this which constitutes the risk."[8] Van Bavel brings together two key issues. First, that God as Love (1 John 4:16) is diffusive of himself, that is to say, God wishes to share existence, a key traditional element in Christian theology. Second, this leads him to speak of God's self-limitation. Thus, omnipotence is understood as "allowing the other to be."[9] Allowing the other to be, allowing creation to be, necessarily limits what is understood by God's omnipotence. God chooses to be limited in creating. This is often termed as kenotic/self-emptying theology, in which the accent shifts from an Almighty God philosophically construed to a God who is Almighty-in-love. This is how Passionist priest-theologian Robin Ryan, following this line of thought, puts it:

> There is a completeness to this inner life of God that precludes the necessity of creation. Yet believers can envision creation as the free, gracious outpouring of this divine life that brings the non-divine into existence and continually sustains it. The God who *is* loving relationship in God's very being freely enters into a loving relationship with every creature. With Karl Rahner we can envision the gift of creation in light of God's intention to offer grace, to communicate Godself to men and women. As Rahner puts it, "God wishes to communicate himself, to pour forth the love which he himself is. That is the first and last of his real plans and hence of his real world too." This is the deepest meaning of reality; it is the "logic" at the heart of the universe.[10]

Of course, this leads us to the question: Could God not have made a better world than this? The answer in the logic of traditional

8. Van Bavel, "Where Is God When Human Beings Suffer?," 144.
9. Van Bavel, "Where Is God When Human Beings Suffer?," 144.
10. Ryan, *God and the Mystery of Human Suffering*, 300–301.

theology would be "Yes." So, Van Bavel asks if such a better world would be *this* world, however. His answer is "No," in line with the reflections of John Cottingham above. The world as we experience it here and now, reflecting the laws of physics and chemistry that regulate existence, could not be different. Furthermore, Van Bavel points out that when we go on to reflect on suffering, "all attention is focused on the negative dimension of our existence" in such a way as to overlook all the positive sides to existence—reconciliation, sunrises and sunsets, healing and comfort, feasting and joy, friendship, beauty and so on.[11]

Continuing to think about the meaning of divine omnipotence Van Bavel (along with many others) considers that we have allowed Greek philosophical categories to be more ultimate than the Scriptures. In any human conversation or exchange there is always an ultimate backdrop, conscious or unconscious, upon which everything finally depends. We might refer to this with the traditional term "metaphysics." As the Christian tradition is handed on, it necessarily negotiates its way through the thickets of thinking present in every generation. In the earliest Christian tradition various forms of Greek philosophy provided the dominant horizon, and ineluctably there developed a certain tension between Hellenistic thinking and the scriptural narrative. In this lengthy quotation from Van Bavel we find a crisp description of the tension. This is what Van Bavel has to say:

> In Greek philosophy, the divine first principle is often represented as uninvolved with the created order, as impervious to suffering. The divine principle does indeed set everything in motion, but it remains itself unmoved, since, as the fullness of being, it cannot be subject to change. The question which immediately arises here is whether one can regard self-absorption and all absence of relation as perfections. Although the Greek idea of God strongly influenced early Christian thought, it is not in harmony with the biblical view of God. The Bible always sees God in active relationship with humanity and the world. That relationship is not viewed as incompatible

11. Van Bavel, "Where Is God When Human Beings Suffer?," 147.

> with the notion of omnipotence. The contradiction is not to be found here but on the part of those who insist on God's omnipotence and, at the same time, steadfastly reject the notion that he can enter into relationship (he can do everything except this—that is, enter into a relationship of love). Love, at least as we have experienced it, is to be always involved with others, either by sharing our lives with them or by sharing in their lives. Can we think of God as in some sense less than a human being? If God is love, then he must be involvement at its highest. If he is such, it is not odd that he is affected by human suffering, and that he shares in the legitimate joys and the suffering of innocent people.[12]

This admittedly provocative passage places the biblical understanding of God squarely in the arena of human suffering, not above it nor beyond it.

Some may ask: Is this not a cheap reconciliation between God and suffering? In de-throning omnipotence, as it were, have we not reduced God to our own level, to the level of human suffering? Van Bavel takes this objection seriously and responds to it by making three points from the scriptural perspective. "First, God is opposed to all suffering which people cause one another, all horrible and senseless suffering. Secondly, in God there is not the suffering powerlessness which is characteristic of humanity. We must not elevate the chaos of our history into a perpetual process in God himself." Finally, he judges that in Jesus we encounter the suffering God in the most intense fashion. "His suffering was not redemptive because he was tortured; it was redemptive because it was the final consequence of his loving commitment to others. Only love, not pain, is redemptive."[13]

12. Van Bavel, "Where Is God When Human Beings Suffer?," 140.

13. Van Bavel, "Where Is God When Human Beings Suffer?," 150–51.

CONCLUSION

Theologians and believers who hold on to what has become known as the "classical" view of God will be unhappy with and opposed to those who think like Van Bavel. They will prefer the understanding of God as omnipotent and impassible, all-mighty and incapable of suffering. It seems to me that as there is no revealed philosophy or metaphysics and if a certain priority is given to the scriptural perspective, then the point of view articulated by Van Bavel and so many other contemporary thinkers is very persuasive.

4

The Law of Retribution and the Lament Psalms

When we attempt to make sense of anything at all, and to utter the sense we have made, we imitate the creating Word of God himself, and we celebrate the order and coherence of the world which that Word has called into being. In that sense, every scientific theory, every mathematical formula, every historical paper, is a liturgical text, and the chanting of the Psalms merely makes explicit the fundamental celebration of meaning and coherence without which we would hardly be human at all. . . . We alone of all created things have taken the measure of mortality, we alone of all the creatures know that we are dying. We sing to the light in the midst of a darkness which we know will one day devour us.

—Eamon Duffy[1]

The psalmist shows himself to be a theologian of Presence. He has so fully cultivated a quotidian communion with the Lord

1. Duffy, *Walking to Emmaus*, 149–50.

of the covenant made with the chosen people that he proclaims unashamedly the mystery of his reason for living. . . . He divulges the most profound secret of his inward life. Theology is inseparable from psychology.

—Samuel Terrien[2]

THE CENTRALITY OF THE BABYLONIAN EXILE (587–538 BCE)

The history of Israel as this is provided for us in the books of the Old Testament is far from straightforward. Scholars tell us that a key period for the composition of the Old Testament is the event known as the Babylonian exile. The historical facts about the exile are these: The people are now without their monarchy (including the king, the court, and the administration), without the temple in Jerusalem, and without their land. These were key factors that had an enormous impact on their identity. The "textual" fact, if we may put it like that, is that in all probability this is the period when much of the Old Testament, perhaps especially the Torah, Psalms, and some of the Prophets, were edited much as we have them now. The theological fact is that the exilic community coming to terms with all that their exile meant threw into high relief the traditional "law of retribution."

THE LAW OF RETRIBUTION

The law of retribution might be summarized as follows: "There is a strong instinct in humans to seek the reasons for their suffering and one reason that often emerges is that we have done something wrong and so are getting what we deserve."[3] Briefly put, the just are rewarded and the wicked are punished. Effectively this means that we are responsible for all that happens to us, the good and the bad.

2. Terrien, *Psalms*, 94.

3. Harrington, *Why Do We Suffer?*, 15.

This law of retribution is found throughout the Torah and the historical books as a key to interpreting the history of Israel from Abraham to the exile of 587 BCE. The righteous are rewarded and the wicked are punished, so Israel's exile must be a punishment for Israel's sins.

In the Torah and the historical books, the Book of Deuteronomy plays a pivotal role. It is a kind of preamble to the historical books. In Deuteronomy 30:15–18 life and prosperity are promised to those who keep the commandments of Israel's covenant with God. Death and adversity are the lot of those who turn away from God and seek other gods:

> See, I have set before you today life and prosperity, death and adversity. If you obey the commandments of the LORD your God that I am commanding you today, by loving the LORD your God, walking in his ways, and observing his commandments, decrees, and ordinances, then you shall live and become numerous, and the LORD your God will bless you in the lands that you are entering to possess. But if your heart turns away and you do not hear, but are led astray to bow down to other gods and serve them, I declare to you today that you shall perish; you shall not live long in the land that you are crossing the Jordan to enter and possess. (Deut 30:15–18)

This text was most likely composed either after the exile of 587 BCE, or not long before it, when the exile seemed to be imminent. The text was then projected back to Moses.

> It was an attempt by the Deuteronomistic editor(s) to make sense out of what had happened in Israel's history and to provide a program for the renewal of Israel as God's people. From the perspective of Deuteronomy, Israel suffers because it failed to worship the Lord God properly and failed to keep God's commandments, and Israel prospers only when it observes God's law (the Torah). . . . The cultural, political, social, and economic factors that are so important in modern historiography are of secondary interest at best.[4]

4. Harrington, *Why Do We Suffer?*, 22.

The great prophets of Israel build on the law of retribution, and they challenge the people to repent, warning of coming disaster. Repentance, however, is not forthcoming. All the prophets agree in invoking the law of retribution as a way of explaining the greatest catastrophes in the history of Israel. At the same time, they refuse to give sin and suffering the last word, and they hold out hope of repentance and restoration for Israel, for example, Isaiah 7; 11:1–9; Jeremiah 31:31–34; Ezekiel 40–48. The Jeremiah passage is especially illuminating. The prophet has acknowledged Israel's sin and the consequent catastrophes, but in this particular text we find comfort and hope, comfort and hope that refuses ultimacy to the ironclad logic of the law of retribution:

> The days are surely coming, says the LORD, when I will make a new covenant with the house of Israel and the house of Judah. It will not be like the covenant that I made with their ancestors when I took them by the hand to bring them out of the land of Egypt—a covenant that they broke, though I was their husband, says the LORD. But this is the covenant that I will make with the house of Israel after those days, says the LORD: I will put my law within them, and I will write it on their hearts; and I will be their God, and they shall be my people. No longer shall they teach one another, or say to each other, "Know the LORD," for they shall all know me, from the least of them to the greatest, says the LORD; for I will forgive their iniquity, and remember their sin no more.

Here the evil consequences of Israel's refusal to live into the demands of the covenant with God do not have the final say. God has the final say, and that final say is both comfort and hope. The law of retribution in that sense has been put aside.

THE BOOK OF PSALMS: LAMENT AND PRAISE

Psalms has been prayed by both Jews and Christians for thousands of years. That fact alone underscores its importance. Old Testament scholar and theologian Ellen F. Davis writes of Psalms: "We do not know who wrote them or, in most cases, how they were used. . . . What emerges clearly in these poems is often a vividly drawn emotional condition, and always a certain web of relations—to God, to other humans, and even to nonhuman creatures—that constitutes the world in which the psalmist claims a place."[5] It is especially the web of relations with God that is our concern here as we continue to explore the theological meaning of evil and suffering in human life. I think it is fair to say that this is a constant theme of Psalms. To understand that theme, however, we must first understand something about the Psalter as a whole. The Book of Psalms has a fivefold division, imitating the Torah, the Five Books of Moses, with the first two psalms as introductory to the entire Psalter.

Book 1 = 3–41

Book 2 = 42–72

Book 3 = 73–89

Book 4 = 90–106

Book 5 = 107–50

At the end of each book, there is a short hymn of praise that brings that book to a conclusion:

> Psalm 41:13. "Blessed be the LORD, the God of Israel, from everlasting to everlasting. Amen and Amen."
>
> Psalm 72:18–19. "Blessed be the LORD, the God of Israel, who alone does wondrous things. Blessed be his glorious name forever; may his glory fill the whole earth. Amen and Amen."
>
> Psalm 89:52. "Blessed be the LORD forever. Amen and Amen."
>
> Psalm 106:48. "Blessed be the LORD, the God of Israel, from everlasting to everlasting. And let all the people say, 'Amen.' Praise the LORD!"
>
> Psalm 150:6. "Let everything that breathes praise the LORD! Praise the LORD!"

5. Davis, *Opening Israel's Scriptures*, 312.

Arguably, these notes of praise function as regulative for the Book of Psalms.

> Most of the great Christian teachers have devoted much energy to expounding as well as singing the Psalms. Origen, Chrysostom, Augustine, Thomas Aquinas, Luther, and Calvin are together in this. It is no accident that in each of them lifelong use and interpretation of the Psalms went together with passionate wrestling with key doctrines and the knowledge of God. Aquinas even said that the Psalms contain all theology in the mode of praise.[6]

The praise of God runs throughout the entire Psalter, and especially in the first collection, Psalms 3–41, and so we find Psalms 8, 19, 29, and 35 praising God for his power and steadfast love. My argument here is that the constancy of this theme of praise provides the interpretive context for understanding what are known as the psalms of lament.[7] The lament psalms are the largest category among the canonical Psalms: 3, 5, 6, 7, 13, 17, 22, 25, 26, 27, 28, 31, 35, 38, 39, 42, 43, 51, 53, 55, 56, 57, 61, 63, 64, 69, 70, 71, 86, 88, 102, 109, 120, 130, 140, 141, 142, 143. When we read or pray through these psalms we understand in our bones exactly what lament is all about. Thinking about these lament psalms we may say:

- *Psychologically* they help sufferers get in touch with their emotions and address God directly and without religious censorship.

6. Hardy and Ford, *Jubilate*, 36–37.

7. Nowell writes, "The Psalter contains more laments than any other genre. Is this because we pray more when we're in trouble? Or because our sufferings are each unique? Or perhaps just because life is hard? In any case, the structure of the laments teaches us how to deal with difficulty: take it straight to God. There is no skulking in corners in the lament. We cry out clearly and powerfully about whatever is troubling us: sorrow, pain, enemies, and even death. Nothing is too raw to be brought to God in prayer!" (*Pleading, Cursing, Praising*, 21).

- *Socially* they encourage sufferers, often feeling alone and misunderstood, to recognize that they belong to a tradition of suffering and the community of sufferers. No one is alone.
- *Theologically* they help sufferers face the reality of suffering and articulate their own questions.

This is even the case, at least to some extent, with Psalm 88, sometimes known as the gloomiest psalm:

> O Lord, God of my salvation,
> when, at night, I cry out in your presence,
> Let my prayer come before you;
> incline your ear to my cry.
> For my soul is full of troubles,
> and my life draws near to Sheol.
> I am counted among those who go down to the Pit;
> I am like those who have no help
> like those forsaken among the dead,
> like the slain that lie in the grave,
> like those whom you remember no more,
> for they are cut off from your hand.
> You have put me in the depths of the Pit,
> in the regions dark and deep.
> Your wrath lies heavy upon me,
> and you overwhelm me with all your waves.
> You have caused my companions to shun me;
> you have made me a thing of horror to them.
> I am shut in that I cannot escape;
> my eye grows dim through sorrow.
> Every day I call on you, O Lord;
> I spread out my hands to you.
> Do you work wonders for the dead?
> Do the shades rise up to praise you?
> Is your steadfast love declared in the grave,
> or your faithfulness in Abaddon?
> Are your wonders known in the darkness,
> or your saving help in the land of forgetfulness?
> But I, O Lord, cry out to you;
> in the morning my prayer comes before you.
> O Lord, why do you cast me off?

> Why do you hide your face from me?
> Wretched and close to death from my youth up, I suffer
> your terrors;
> I am desperate.
> Your wrath has swept over me;
> your dread assaults destroy me.
> They surrounded me like a flood all day long;
> from all sides they close in on me.
> You have caused friend and neighbor to shun me;
> my companions are in darkness.

Let's turn to two of my favorite commentators on Psalms for assistance in understanding the text. From John H. Eaton:

> Much of the imagery for suffering comes from ancient poetic tradition depicting Sheol, the universal tomb or home of the dead, imagined as a place of darkness, silence, and utter weakness beneath the subterranean waters. . . . In the first line of the psalm God is addressed as "God of my salvation." . . . Again the bond, the commitment of goodwill, the experience of grace. The prayer to this Savior rises night and day, a cry and a supplication which strives to rise from the depths to reach his holy throne. This is the nature of all that will follow. Utterly tragic as it seems, it is all directed to him who alone can save. Underlying all is a hidden but massive foundation of faith and hope.[8]

From Artur Weiser: "The psalmist's repeated references to the prayers he has offered, and indeed the psalm itself, are proof that he cannot let God go in spite of the distress experienced in his prayers, which, after all, is the deepest cause of his despair."[9]

The psalm is a sustained and relentless complaint, with very little if any confession of trust in God, challenging God to do something. There is no thanksgiving in the text and it ends in great darkness: "You have caused friend and neighbor to shun me; my companions are in darkness." But perhaps we can say more with biblical scholar Daniel Harrington:

8. Eaton, *Psalms*, 314.

9. Weiser, *Psalms*, 586.

> Besides being known as the gloomiest psalm, Psalm 88 is often called a dialogue with an absent God. The psalmist calls out to a God who appears to have abandoned him and to be hiding from him. Yet the absent God is still somehow present—present enough to be addressed in prayer, to be criticized, and to be angry at. Even though the psalmist feels that God has given up on him, he is not willing to give up on God. God exists. There is no speculative atheism or agnosticism here. God is the problem, and God had better do something about it. It is relatively easy to believe in God when things go well and life proceeds in an orderly way. In Psalm 88, however, we have someone whose life is a mess and God seems very far away. Somehow and from somewhere the psalmist is able to express a firm faith in God while challenging God and expressing anger at God.[10]

Psalm 44 is another example of a lament psalm and it, too, challenges the theology of retribution. According to one commentator, however, this particular psalm adds another dimension of meaning: "Although the psalm does not propose a clear alternative explanation for suffering, it does make the enigmatic assertion that God's people suffer 'for the sake of' God."[11] Reading through the psalm we may divide it up as follows:

Verse 1	heading
Verses 2–4	recollection of God's saving deeds
Verses 5–9	expressions of trust in God
Verses 10–17	the present disaster, the defeat in battle of God's people
Verses 18–23	a protest of innocence and faithfulness
Verses 24–27	prayer for deliverance

It remains unclear what the military defeat is behind the psalm. Applying the law of retribution, one expects the psalmist's

10. Harrington, *Why Do We Suffer?*, 10.

11. Martin, "Psalm 44," 18.

acknowledgment on behalf of the people that it is their lack of faithfulness to their covenant with God that is the cause of their defeat. Then notice verses 17–18: "All this has come upon us, *yet we have not forgotten you, or been false to your covenant. Our heart has not turned back, nor have our steps departed from your way*" (my italics). The claim is strong, that is, that the people's defeat is not due to their sin, their lack of covenantal faithfulness. In point of fact, the psalmist goes on to assert in verse 22, "Because of you we are being killed all day long, and accounted as sheep for the slaughter."

CONCLUSION

Standing back and thinking about evil and suffering, I think we can say that in some cases the law of retribution seems true. For example, in cases where I do something stupid and suffer as a result. Obviously, however, in cases of egregious suffering such as the Shoah/Holocaust this does not work. Returning again to Scripture, scholar and theologian Daniel Harrington has put it so well:

> One need only look at a daily newspaper to see terrible suffering being brought about by human sin and the happiness that results from just and loving conduct. Furthermore, when persons come to see the real reasons for their suffering and recognize that they can do something about them, they frequently begin to take responsibility for their harmful behaviors and seek to change the direction of their lives. However, the law of retribution does not always prove true. . . . Many experiences of suffering are so complex that they defy the easy explanation that the law of retribution gives.[12]

Finally, the note of praise and trust in God is never absent from the Book of Psalms, even in lament. Acknowledging this, could we say that the praise of God is the proper, final ecology for lament?

12. Harrington, *Why Do We Suffer?*, 28.

5

The Books of Job and Qoheleth

Job is a poetic tale that undermines and mocks all stock responses to suffering.

—Michael Paul Gallagher[1]

INTRODUCTION

Why do bad things happen to us? The law of retribution, examined in chapter 3, is based on the idea that "You reap what you sow!" Our suffering is brought about by ourselves. While this may be true of some kinds of suffering in life, there are many situations in which it is simply not true. There are too many experiences of suffering that will not allow this kind of easy explanation. The Old Testament's Book of Job in particular disallows the law of retribution and prompts reflection, and so "the book of Job may be said to represent a crisis in the wisdom tradition, arising from the realization that some of the most hallowed assumptions are proven false by experience."[2]

1. Gallagher, *Human Poetry of Faith*, 53.
2. Collins, *Introduction to the Hebrew Bible*, 537.

THE BOOK OF JOB

The Book of Job was written after the Babylonian exile (587–538 BCE). Job may well be a figure symbolic of Israel's collective suffering in the exile of the sixth century BCE as the exiles in Babylon tried to come to terms with the sufferings that had overtaken them. Job is presented as a pious, devout, and prosperous man, almost a living saint. The satan, the prosecuting attorney in God's court, proposes to God that Job's piety is founded on the fact that everything has gone well for Job, but that piety will crumble if Job is confronted with suffering. "Then Satan answered the LORD, 'Does Job fear God for nothing? Have you not put a fence around him and his house and all that he has, on every side? You have blessed the work of his hands, and his possessions have increased in the land. But stretch out your hand now, and touch all that he has, and he will curse you to your face'" (Job 1:9–11). God then gives permission to the satan to test Job by taking away from him all that makes life good. His children perish, his wealth is removed, and he himself falls prey to a dreadful illness. It is difficult to disagree with Old Testament scholar Roland Murphy when he describes the interview between God and the satan in the heavenly court in these terms:

> The scene in the heavenly court may be imaginative, but it raises a nagging question: What kind of a God is this who is willing to prove a point of honor by sorely afflicting a faithful servant? The scene presupposes an understanding of God that the modern reader may be loath to share. Ancient Israel obviously did not have such qualms. There was a dark side, or underside, to God that was simply accepted. This dark side resulted from the worldview that attributed to a divine agency all that happens, evil as well as good.[3]

Murphy seems to me to be quite right here, even as he insists that the scene is imaginative, and that we need to allow for development in thinking about God.

3. Murphy, *Tree of Life*, 36.

Eliphaz, Bildad, and Zophar are friends of Job. They come to reason with him about his plight, but they are stalwart defenders of the traditional view of the law of retribution. So extreme is Job's situation that they remain in silence for a week. Job later comments that silence in point of fact is their only wisdom: "If you would only keep silent, that would be your wisdom!" (Job 13:5). The friends grow progressively vehement in their indictment of Job as the book goes on. "They are not willing to leave a margin of uncertainty, to admit limits to their understanding, to write after each of their theses, 'If God so wills.' All the workings of divine providence must be clear to them, explicit, mathematical. They have fallen victims to the occupational hazard of theologians: they forget they are dealing with mystery."[4]

Eliphaz, Bildad, and Zophar are non-Jews, like Job himself. The three friends lecture Job directly and at length, but interestingly they never speak *to* God. By way of contrast, Job often turns *to* God in the book. Job argues with God, and even if he cannot find God (23:8–9), he never stops yearning for a confrontation (9:32–35; 13:3, 16, 22; 16:18–22; 31:35–37). We read in Job 23: "O that I knew where I might find him, that I might come even to his dwelling! . . . If I go forward, he is not there; or backward, I cannot perceive him; on the left he hides, and I cannot behold him; I turn to the right, but I cannot see him." The three friends are locked into their rational reflections while Job, in great suffering, continues in his spiritual quest of God.

The book reaches its dramatic climax in the appearance of God, who speaks as "the voice from the whirlwind." "Then the Lord answered Job out of the whirlwind: 'Who is this that darkens counsel by words without knowledge? Gird up your loins like a man, I will question you, and you shall declare to me'" (Job 38:1). Now follow two speeches from God. The first speech (chapters 38–39) reflects on God's power over creation. It is a magnificent series of questions put by God to Job underscoring not only God's transcendent power but also his care for his creation. The speech has its effect; it reduces Job to silence: "See, I am of small account;

4. MacKenzie and Murphy, "Job," 467.

what shall I answer you? I lay my hand on my mouth" (Job 40:4). The second speech (40:6—41:34) focuses on God's power and care for Behemoth and Leviathan—two mighty monsters. Behemoth is probably a description of the hippopotamus, "probably written from hearsay rather than from observation," and Leviathan is "the mythological monster of chaos."[5] The questions posed by God in these two speeches totally overwhelm Job, who is left in silent awe at God's power.

However, we may say more.

> The presupposition of God's speeches is that the Lord somehow reveals himself in creation, for the result of this encounter is Job's transformation. The Lord's questions add little to Job's fund of knowledge, but they do leave him changed. . . . It is enough for Job; vision has replaced hearsay. Job's experience of God in the theophany works the transformation that the lectures of the friends could not accomplish.[6]

Job is transformed through this experience of encounter with God—silent, yes, but transformed. Let's turn to the marvelous passage in Job 42:1–6:

> Then Job answered the LORD: "I know that you can do all things, and that no purpose of yours can be thwarted. [You said] 'Who is this that hides counsel without knowledge?' Therefore, I have uttered what I did not understand, things too wonderful for me, which I did not know. [You said] 'Hear, and I will speak; I will question you, and you declare to me.' I had heard of you by the hearing of the ear, but now my eye sees you; therefore I despise myself, and repent in dust and ashes.

In this passage God's words spoken to Job in 38:2 are repeated—"Who is this that darkens counsel by words without knowledge?"—and Job is transformed. Job refuses to impose on God his own very limited human understanding, and through personal

5. McKenzie, *Dictionary of the Bible*, 87, 505.

6. Murphy, *Tree of Life*, 43.

encounter he has reached a point of what can best be called mystical transformation. Michael Paul Gallagher put it so well:

> God eventually speaks "from the heart of the tempest," but not as a philosopher on the problem of pain. Nothing is said about suffering or about innocence or guilt. The issue of "why" gives way to the issue of "who" God is. . . . The healing moment comes not through what God says but through the transforming presence of God.[7]

CONTRAST WITH QOHELETH

"If Job is a story of a man whose relationship to God drove him into a whirlwind of spiritual turmoil, the author of the book of Ecclesiastes, Qoheleth, portrays himself as a very different and somewhat enigmatic character; though his attitude to much in the religious tradition which nurtured him is equally radical."[8] The Book of Job questions traditional wisdom about suffering based on the traditional belief about the law of retribution. The book of Ecclesiastes/Qoheleth is much the same. While commentators on Qoheleth vary greatly in their understanding of the text, the majority consider it to be from the second century BCE.

> Even a quick reading of Qoheleth senses a language and tone in a minor key, giving the unmistakable impression that someone is struggling intellectually/mentally. Words and expressions like "unhappy business, sore affliction, grievous ill, evil, ill, vexation, toil, wearisome, chasing after the wind, under the sun," and the almost untranslatable, yet thematic *hebel* (often translated as "vanity") are among Qoheleth's favorites.[9]

That quick reading would also register the fact of the first-person personal pronoun "I" throughout the book. The author is a thinker reaching through his own personal experience of life within the

7. Gallagher, *Human Poetry of Faith*, 54–55.
8. Davidson, *Courage to Doubt*, 184.
9. Gigliotti, "Portrait of an Artist in Pain," 74.

cultural and theological context of his inherited Judaism. The intellectual and skeptical struggle to come to terms with traditional beliefs reaches its high point in this book, making the book something of a controversy in early Judaism. "In the first century CE the rival schools of Shammai and Hillel were divided [about Qoheleth]. The more conservative school of Shammai rejected it, but the Hillelites prevailed. Objections continued to be raised against the book as late as the fourth century CE because of its lack of coherence and its radical questioning of tradition."[10]

"The sun rises and the sun goes down; back it returns to its place and rises there again. The wind blows south, the wind blows north, round and round it goes and returns full-circle. All streams run into the sea, yet the sea never overflows; back to the place from which the streams ran they return to run again" (Qoheleth 1:5–7). Again and again the author insists that life is what it is, and that there is little point in getting uptight or complaining about it. Put in a colloquial vein, "Life is hard and then you die." Qoheleth is particularly skeptical about life after death. In the ancient world and indeed in today's world some consider that one might live on by being remembered for one's good name of what one accomplished. "Qoheleth underlines the futility of such hope. Only a few people are remembered, and even they may not be remembered accurately. Qoheleth insists that there is no transcendence of death and no way out of the cyclical existence in which humanity is trapped."[11]

The conclusion of the Scottish Old Testament scholar Robert Davidson, contrasting Job and Qoheleth, seems right on the mark:

> Whereas the author of Job insists in struggling to save faith in a just world order, Qoheleth gives up the struggle. It doesn't make sense, cries Job, but it *must* make sense. It doesn't make sense, says Qoheleth, accept that it doesn't make sense. . . . So the book of Job climaxes in God speaking to Job; and Qoheleth ends, where he

10. Collins, *Introduction to the Hebrew Bible*, 537.

11. Collins, *Introduction to the Hebrew Bible*, 539–40.

> begins, with a silent God, and the whole of life described as completely *hebel* (chasing after the wind).[12]

CONCLUSION

Perhaps a systematic theologian might add a further interpretive comment to this contrast of Job and Qoheleth based on the work of Friedrich von Hügel (1852–1925), *The Mystical Element of Religion*, first published in 1909. As a theologian, von Hügel is usually considered a participant in the Catholic "Modernist Crisis" of the late nineteenth and early twentieth centuries.[13] Von Hügel posits three necessary dimensions of faith. First is the institutional dimension: We come to faith through others—parents, environment, teachers, clergy, etc.—all understood broadly as the institutions and necessary structures of human life. The cumulative effect of the institutional dimension of religion is mainly (but not only!) a passive social-cultural-religious formation in which personal intellectual judgment and critical reason is not the fore. Second is the intellectual dimension. This is the point in the life cycle when people begin to ask probing questions about the faith they received. Critical reasoning is now in place and is applied to the multiple layers of formation that the individual has received. Often it is marked by an either/or approach to intellectual judgment Third is the mystical-transformative dimension. This is a both/and approach that recognizes the values of the institutional stage of development while at the same time acknowledges the necessity for personal experience and critique. However, this stage goes much further for the religious person. At this point the person becomes aware of the permeative presence of God and lets themselves be transformed gradually by that awareness. Accepting von Hügel's developmental approach to religion, could we see Qoheleth struggling with the second dimension/the intellectual

12. Davidson, *Courage to Doubt*, 201.

13. For von Hügel in context, see Cummings, *Popes, Councils, and Theology*, 97–100.

pretty much either/or thinking, and Job moving into the mystical/transformative dimension both/and thinking?

6

The Mystical Vision of The Cross

Christian thought about suffering cannot be reduced to explaining it away, in however philosophically sophisticated a way. It must rather embrace the fact that suffering lies at the heart of its formative story.

—Frances M. Young[1]

INTRODUCTION

Towards the end of chapter 5 we introduced some of the ideas of Baron Friedrich von Hügel (1852–1925), the lay Catholic theologian who famously spoke of three necessary dimensions of Catholicism: the institutional, the intellectual, and the mystical. These dimensions of Catholicism, and arguably of all religious traditions, hang together and offer an approach to the experience of evil and suffering.

The institutional dimension rightly makes use of all possible means to alleviate the experience of evil and suffering—science

1. Young, "Suffering," 689.

and technology, medicine, planning to reduce the effects of climate change, agricultural planning to counter famine, personal financial contributions, etc. The intellectual dimension strives to understand as best we can the roots and causes of suffering through philosophical and theological analysis and struggle. The mystical dimension recognizes the Mystery that is God through entering ever more deeply into communion with God through prayer (personal and liturgical), sacramental participation, especially in Eucharist, and regular moments of adoration and praise.

One version of the mystical dimension that was popular especially among Catholics in the past was offering up suffering with Christ and/or looking at Christ on the cross. This kind of mystical engagement enabled many people to cope with their sufferings. It often took the form of a daily prayer. There are variants to this prayer but the substance of it is as follows: "O Jesus, through the most pure heart of Mary, I offer you all my prayers, works, joys, and sufferings of this day in union with the Holy Sacrifice of the Mass throughout the world. I offer them for all the intentions of your Sacred Heart: the salvation of souls, reparation for sin, and the reunion of all Christians." While there is much theological value in this prayer, I am unsure that it works now as well as it has done in the past. In part this is because, like many Catholic prayers and devotionals, it has fallen by the wayside in recent decades. It is no longer remembered and recited on a daily basis, and so it no longer enjoys the powerful support it once had. There is, however, another reason why the prayer is no longer persuasive for so many today, a reason captured well by the English Catholic theologian Paul Murray:

> For my own part, I do in fact consider the constellation of ideas which tends to lie behind the spirituality of "offering our suffering up" to be unhealthy and damaging, distorted and distorting. I also, however, hold—both on account of its inescapable role in human life and on account of its central relationship with the Christian tradition—that we urgently need to find an alternative, non-pathological and convincing way of positively and

> actively integrating suffering into our spiritual lives, in a manner which flows from the heart of the tradition.[2]

One can readily see how "offering suffering up" could become pathological in the sense that it might encourage devout people to seek out as much suffering as possible, confirming what could only be understood as a distorted understanding of God. Returning to the thought of Paul Murray for a moment, we find a much more persuasive (and traditional) understanding of God. Let me quote him at some length:

> Given that the Trinity is the fully actualized act of joyous love, in which there is no lack, no un-actualized potential, and no possibility of diminishment, this divine dynamic of life-giving, self-giving should not be understood as a self-emptying but as always being from fullness unto fullness in the one eternal act of God's Trinitarian love. It genuinely is "the gift which keeps on giving" and without any diminishment in the process. On the contrary, as the life-giving, self-giving that is the inexhaustibly abundant joyous love of divine life, it is always generative, whether in the Trinity, in creation, in redemption, or in consummation. . . . We are called to enter into and to live out of this divine dynamic of life-giving, self-giving—this one eternal act of joyous love—in and through the details and circumstances of our lives and to become there living prayers and effective channels of God's sustaining and transforming being-with creation and the cost it entails. . . . This learning to become living prayers and effective channels of the Trinity's sustaining, transforming being-with creation is the fundamental schooling for eternity . . . which is taking place in every moment of our lives.[3]

These words of Murray's are both profound and worthy of careful re-reading and meditating. Although Murray indicates in his essay that his position has deep roots in the entirety of the Christian tradition, especially in the Augustinian-Thomist tributaries, it seems

2. Murray, "Living Sacrifice," 190.

3. Murray, "Living Sacrifice," 202–3.

to me that it finds exemplification in the theology of St. Paul and to that I shall now turn.

TURNING TO THE PAULINE COSMIC-MYSTICAL VISION

Colossians 1:15–20

> He is the image of the invisible God, the first-born of all creation; for in him all things were created, in heaven and on earth, visible and invisible, whether thrones or dominions or principalities or authorities—all things were created through him and for him. He is before all things, and in him all things hold together. He is the head of the body, the church; he is the beginning, the first-born from the dead, that in everything he might be pre-eminent. For in him all the fullness of God was pleased to dwell, and through him to reconcile to himself all things, whether on earth or in heaven, making peace by the blood of his cross.

The entire cosmos for Paul is to be seen and understood through and in Jesus Christ. This is an astonishing claim, that every single aspect of creation is originated through Christ, finds its central meaning in Christ, and Christ is mystically at the heart of creation, transforming and sustaining it. Language begins to fail here, almost to break down, and adoration seems the only adequate posture. This means that the human person and the entirety of creation can be rightly understood only from a Christ-centered viewpoint.

Now think of such Pauline texts as:

> 1 Corinthians 3:17: "If anyone destroys God's temple, God will destroy him. For God's temple is holy, and that temple you are."

> 1 Corinthians 6:19: "Do you not know that your body is a temple of the Holy Spirit within you, which you have from God?"

In both texts "you" is plural in Greek, not singular. In these texts St. Paul is telling the Corinthian-Christian community that they are the temple of God. In Paul's time the Jerusalem temple was still standing and for Jews it was the holiest place on earth, the very dwelling place of God. Now Paul transfers something of that meaning to the Christian community itself. They are the very dwelling place of God since they have God's Spirit within them. For example, consider Galatians 2:20: "I live, no longer I, but Christ lives in me." Think also of Philippians 1:21: "For to me life is Christ." Could we say that Paul (and so also ourselves) not only identifies with Christ but somehow, ineffably, is Christ? As already noted, language is breaking down here as intellectual clarity, always necessary, yields to mystical paradox. Or, in Friedrich von Hügel's understanding, the intellectual dimension is yielding to the mystical dimension.

This mystical faith-union of the believer with Christ is found in many Pauline passages. Sometimes, it is expressed very simply as being "in Christ." "Christ is personally united with his people in such a way that they become his 'body.' He is actually present in and through them. . . . Consequently, he manifests his identity to the world through this complex corporate reality. . . . The Church really is the Body of Christ, because Christ lives in us."[4]

This fundamental mystical unity gets expressed using the Greek word *syn*, "with, along with, together with." Consider the following examples:

Rom 6:4	*synthaptein*	to be buried with
Rom 6:6	*systarousthai*	to be crucified with
Rom 6:8	*syzein*	to live with
Rom 8:17	*sympaschein*	to suffer with
	syndoxazein	to be glorified with

4. Hays, "Story of God's Son," 195.

	sygkleronomoi	to be joint heirs with
2 Cor 7:3	*synapothanein*	to die with
Col 2:12	*synthaptein*	to be buried with
	synegerein	to be raised with
Col 2:13	*syzoopoiein*	to be made alive with

In the light of these passages, and reflecting on all these verbs with *syn*/"with," the mystical identity of the believer with Christ is crystal clear, even as the language is that of paradox. In summary form:

> [Paul] does seem to conceive of the living Christ as more than individual, while still knowing him vividly and distinctly as fully personal. He speaks of Christian life as lived in an area which is Christ; he speaks of Christians as incorporated in him. He thinks of the Christian community as (ideally) a harmoniously co-ordinated living organism like a body, and, on occasion, thinks of Christ as himself the living body of which Christians are limbs.[5]

Now return to Galatians 2:20, linking human suffering to Christ: "I have been crucified with Christ; I live, no longer I, but Christ lives in me; and the life which I now live in the flesh I live by faith in the Son of God, who loved me and gave himself for me." Living as Christ, crucified with Christ. What an immensely challenging phrase! Catholics may not use this particular Pauline phrase with any regularity, but they frequently perform it, as it were, when they make the sign of the cross. This simple action of signing ourselves with the cross of Christ is profoundly significant.

> The sign of the cross as a prayer is not a mere request for help and courage for the little personal crosses we may bear in our own life (all told this certainly is one of its obvious messages). The sign of the cross signifies our participation in the body of the church. The sign throughout history has been an identifying mark of Christianity, its mystical significance connecting each of us with the larger body of the church and with the Crucified Christ.[6]

5. Moule, *Origin of Christology*, 85.
6. Andreopoulos, *Sign of the Cross*, 102.

This language of Paul should not be thought of as overblown or inflated, but rather as paradoxical and yet fully real. The newly baptized Christian has been inserted into Christ, and therefore into the communion of the Trinity, in such a way that Christ becomes his/her most intimate identity. The New Testament scholar Morna Hooker has captured Paul's theology of grace finely when she writes, "Look at Christ and you will see what God is like; look at Christians, and what you should see is what Christ is like."[7] Taking this mystical understanding further with some comments from Rowan Williams:

> Jesus cannot be spoken of simply as an individual in the past. He is not only currently active, but the "kinship group" of which he is the common and defining "ancestor" is here and now open to his agency and growing into a different kind of existence as a result of that agency, which is "appropriated" to its human members, in the sense that what they do and say in the name or persona of Jesus counts as done or said by Jesus.[8]

TURNING TO THE LATIN WEST: AUGUSTINE

This mystical Pauline vision is continued in the tradition, especially by Augustine. For Augustine, Psalms form the very language of confession—and "confession," for him, is the very action that unites us to Christ.[9]

> God could have granted no greater gift to human beings than to cause his Word, through whom he created all things, to be their head, and to fit them to him as his members. He was thus to be Son of God and Son of Man, one God with the Father, one human being with us. The consequence is that when we speak to God in prayer we do not separate the Son from God, and when the body of the Son prays it does not separate its head from itself. The

7. Hooker and Young, *Holiness and Mission*, 13.
8. Williams, *Christ the Heart of Creation*, 55.
9. Grove, *Augustine on Memory*, 59–62.

> one sole savior of his body is our Lord Jesus Christ, the Son of God, who prays for us, prays in us, and is prayed to by us. He prays for us as our priest, he prays in us as our head, and he is prayed to by us as our God.[10]

This is St. Paul paraphrased several centuries later. Continuing with St. Augustine:

> Accordingly, when we hear his voice, we must hearken to it as coming from both head and body; for whatever he suffered, we too suffered in him; and it follows that now that he has ascended into heaven and is seated at the Father's right hand, he still undergoes in the person of the church whatever it may suffer amid the troubles of the world, whether temptations, or hardship or oppression.[11]

TURNING TO THE GREEK EAST: SYMEON THE NEW THEOLOGIAN

St. Symeon the New Theologian (949–1022) wrote,

> We awaken in Christ's body
> as Christ awakens our bodies,
> and my poor hand is Christ, he enters
> my foot, and is infinitely me.
>
> I move my hand, and wonderfully
> my hand becomes Christ, becomes all of him
> (for God is indivisibly
> whole, seamless in his Godhood).
>
> I move my foot, and at once
> he appears like a flash of lightning.
> Do my words seem blasphemous?—Then
> open your heart to him.
>
> And let yourself receive the one
> who is opening to you so deeply.
> For if we genuinely love him,
> we wake up inside Christ's body

10. Augustine, *Exposition of Psalm 85*, 1.
11. Augustine, *Exposition of Psalm 62*, 2.

Where all our body, all over,
every most hidden part of it,
is realized in joy as him,
and he makes us, utterly, real,

And everything that is hurt, everything
that seemed to us dark, harsh, shameful,
maimed, ugly, irreparably
damaged, is in him transformed.

And recognized as whole, as lovely,
and radiant in his light
we awaken as the Beloved
in every last part of our body.[12]

TURNING TO THE MYSTIC BENEDICT OF CANFIELD, OFMCAP

Benedict of Canfield (1563–1610) is a little-known theologian and mystic who conveys this mystical sense of being in Christ in a breathtaking way. This is what he writes in *The Rule of Perfection* (1609):

> Therefore our own pains—insofar as they are not ours but those of Christ—must be deeply respected. How wonderful! And more: our pains are as much to be revered as those of Jesus Christ in His own passion. For if people correctly adore Him with so much devotion in images on the Good Friday cross, why may we not then revere Him on the living cross that we ourselves are?[13]

Behind this overwhelming statement of Benedict's lies the fundamental and unalterable identification of the Christian with Christ. We are by grace, as it were, who Christ is by nature, one in being with the Father. In and through baptism and sustained especially through the Eucharist we are "Christified," and, if Christified, then also "Trinified." Our sufferings are in that sense the sufferings of

12. Cited in Radcliffe, *Take the Plunge*, 161–62.

13. My adaptation of Benedict of Canfield, *Holy Will of God*, 67–71.

Christ. The twentieth-century Dominican theologian Gerald Vann puts it like this: "The death that leads to resurrection is not just a death, but a sacrificial death, *a death turned into an act of love and self-giving*."[14] Sacrifice, or suffering, is here understood as "an act of love and self-giving," not simply something endured but rather actively entered into.

SACRIFICE AS LIFE-GIVING

I have tried to schematize this understanding christologically and in respect of the triune God as follows in these numbered points.[15]

1. Let us begin simultaneously with God and with ourselves. Beginning with God, we note that God is incomprehensible, and therefore, that our language fails. Nonetheless, we read in 1 John 4:16, "God is Love (*agape*), and he who lives in love lives in God and God lives in him." Love is God's best name.
2. So, what is "love"? Love is the process of self-donation/self-giving to/for another and is the highest value-experience that we humans know. Could we say, paraphrasing St. Anselm of Canterbury, that Love is that than which nothing greater can be conceived?
3. Love is necessarily relational. We never simply love, we necessarily love someone or something.
4. In human terms, the agapeic Love that God is is simply inaccessible to us. What it is for the Three-in-One to love is inaccessible to us.
5. Jesus is that Love in human form; in other words, Jesus is divine. Perhaps we could put it like this: There is nothing in God that is not "Jesus-like."

14. Vann, *Pain of Christ*, 60, my italics. Quoted in Murray, "Living Sacrifice," 189–206.

15. An approach to sacrifice very similar to what I am proposing here may be found in Bulgakov, *Eucharistic Sacrifice*. I owe this reference to my colleague Dr. Justin Coyle.

6. The entire life of Jesus may be understood as a process of self-donation/self-giving for others (in preaching and teaching, in healing, in companionship, in foot-washing, and in numerous other ways).
7. Now consider John 13:1: "Having loved his own in the world, he loved them *to the end*" (Greek, *eis telos*; my italics). We might say, Jesus continued to give himself to the end, to the point beyond which one cannot go.
8. Now go to Jesus in John 19:30: "When Jesus had received the wine, he said, 'It is finished'" (Greek, *tetelestai*). To give to the point of death is the *telos*, the "end."
9. In summary: Love is self-donation/self-giving; Love is sacrifice.
10. So, "sacrifice" is what God is.
11. So, "sacrifice" is what we are at our best.

After his sufferings and death, the *telos* of his love/self-giving, Christ was raised into the glory of God. We can then proceed to say that after our sufferings and death, our hope, too, is to be raised into the glory of God. Using slightly different language, the Paschal Mystery of the Lord becomes our paschal mystery too.

Now this does not mean that we should not use all the available aids to alleviate our suffering in this world—medicine, pharmacology, surgical intervention, psychotherapy, etc. Since God is never absent from his creation, God's presence is mediated through such healing processes. God's final healing comes through our resurrection, our participation in Christ's glorious resurrection, and our final communion with the triune God. This vision is what Paul, Augustine, Symeon, and Benedict of Canfield are putting into words. This is the constant tradition of the church.

WHAT HAPPENED TO THIS COSMIC-CORPORATE MYSTICAL VISION?

This glorious vision has never been forgotten—How could it be?—but, in my opinion, two historical events "dislocated" the vision. First, the sixteenth-century Reformations. The Christian world became involved in "intramural" disputes about ecclesiology, the sacramental life, and other such matters. The mystical vision remained, but intellectual energies tended to be engaged in polemics, "doing theology against one another." The second is the period known as the Enlightenment. Think of Immanuel Kant's call, *Sapere aude*, "Think for yourself!" One consequence of the Enlightenment was the massive movement away from *tradition*, when "thinking *for* yourself" became identified with "thinking *by* yourself." Rationalism, individualism, and a sense of being captains of our own ships developed. God-in-Christ-through-the-Spirit, always mystically conjoined with creation/humankind, was relegated to heaven, became a "deity"—that is to say, "some*thing*," even a "divine Something"—rather than the triune Mystery and creative-redeeming Source of all that is, constantly present and inviting communion. This reductive tendency raised questions that, while not new, were put with a greater rational urgency than before: Does this Supreme Something really exist? Can his existence be "proved" rationally? How do you reconcile evil and suffering with a God who is all-good and all-powerful? Philosophical theodicies, in contrast to mystical communion, were on the ascendant.

CONCLUSION

There is no satisfactory rational solution to the problem of evil and suffering. But what if not abandoning our God-given rationality—the intellectual dimension of von Hügel—we enter into the mystical dimension? This mystical dimension, unfolded briefly in this chapter, invites us continually to find ways of alleviating evil and suffering in life, but more wonderfully invites us to see such experiences in terms of our mystical communion with God. If we were constantly to cultivate such a vision, we would be provided with a hope that does not disappoint. The cultivation demands structuring this vision into our everyday lives. "Everything lives, moves, and has its being in God. Everything is grace, everything gift. The world is not random chaos but good. God is not nowhere but everywhere. This may be a hard teaching in times of pain, but the alternative is far worse."[16]

16. Soskice, "Why *Creatio ex Nihilo*?," 52.

7

The Role of Miracles

There are kinds of pietism which are prepared to diagnose the presence of miracles at the drop of a hat. One might call this attitude supernatural reductionism. Those determined to have miracles will have them by hook or by crook.

—Gabriel Daly[1]

INTRODUCTION

In a 2023 movie entitled *The Miracle Club* some women from a working-class Dublin parish set out on pilgrimage to Lourdes. The year is 1967 and each of the women is suffering. The elderly Lily wants to go to Lourdes, something she has always dreamed of doing. Eileen has just discovered a lump in her breast and is hoping for a miraculous cure. Dolly has a young son, Daniel, who is mute and she is hoping that Daniel will speak as a result of the pilgrimage. None of the miracles hoped for takes place, with consequent and inevitable disappointment. However, when they return to Dublin, embittered relationships are healed, suggesting perhaps that this is the real miracle. The movie throws into high relief

1. Daly, *Asking the Father*, 53.

some questions: Do miracles happen in terms of some physical healing or transformation? Are miracles to be understood more symbolically than physically? What is the understanding of God lying behind the quest or the hope for a miracle? Each of these questions is complicated, but we must seek for clarity, not least because when people are suffering we pray for them. But we might want to ask, What we are praying for? A miracle, an acceptance of mortality, or what? To advance our understanding let me turn to some contemporary theologians as they reflect on the nature of the miraculous.[2]

ROWAN D. WILLIAMS

In a small but excellent book, *Tokens of Trust: An Introduction to Christian Belief* (2007), Anglican theologian and former archbishop of Canterbury Rowan Williams (1950–) has a small but powerful treatment of miracles.[3] He opens his discussion with an experience: "Why are some prayers apparently answered and some not? I remember a vivid example from years back, when someone who had been involved in a very upbeat and confident charismatic prayer group asked why God should be thanked for finding parking spaces for members of the prayer group when he couldn't be bothered to sort out the conflict in Northern Ireland."[4] Williams remarks that it is a very good question, but also that, if a genuine answer is to be found, some further thinking about God's almightiness must be undertaken. Without going into all aspects of Williams's model of almightiness, we may grasp the essence of it in these words: "I have been trying to suggest the picture of a God whose almighty power is more of a steady swell of loving presence, always there at work in the center of everything that is, opening the door to a future even when we can see no hope."[5] This

2. I am using here some parts of chapter 7 in my *Miracles in the Christian Tradition*.

3. Williams, *Tokens of Trust*, 43–44.

4. Williams, *Tokens of Trust*, 43–44.

5. Williams, *Tokens of Trust*, 44.

understanding of God's almightiness certainly seems superior to a more capricious view (or what seems a more capricious view) of God's working. "A steady swell of loving presence." And, of course, a steady swell of loving presence that invites human creatures to enter into that swell and to increase its intensity.

Williams goes on to paraphrase/summarize some thinking of St. Augustine on the question of miracle:

> That miracles were really just natural processes speeded up a bit, "fast-forwarded." This may be a bit too simple; but Augustine had got hold of something that many thinkers of the Middle Ages followed through in different ways. If God's action is always at work around us, if it's always "on hand," so to speak, we shouldn't be thinking of God's action and the processes of the world as two competing sorts of thing, jostling for space. But what if there were times when certain bits of the world's processes came together in such a way that the whole cluster of happenings became a bit more open to God's final purposes? What if the world were sometimes a bit more "transparent" to the underlying action of God?[6]

Williams's way of thinking is especially helpful. For Williams,

> God has—mysteriously—made a world in which what human beings do can help or hinder what he achieves at any point in the world's history; when we give him space, through our prayerful consent to and identification with what he wants, things may happen that were otherwise unpredictable. A prejudice against any sort of miracle may be a buried uncertainty about the unfailing presence and action of the Creator, about that burning intensity of divine action that is always around us.[7]

Very briefly, Williams points to the virginal conception of Jesus and to the resurrection of Jesus as illustrative of his integrated point of view. Though he does not develop this point of view at any great length, his remarks are worth noting. "Just what would

6. Williams, *Tokens of Trust*, 44–45.

7. Williams, *Tokens of Trust*, 48–49.

the trust of Mary have had to be like for the door of life itself to open in her body? What must the faith of Jesus and his closeness to God have been that death was unable to close its doors on him and relegate him to the past?"[8] What excellent questions, stimulating us to further probing at the beginning of Jesus' life and at his end, as it were?

THOMAS E. HOSINSKI

Thomas Hosinski (1946–2022) taught theology at the University of Portland in Oregon for many years and, since the time of his doctoral dissertation at the University of Chicago, had a keen interest in reconciling the categories of process philosophy with Catholic theology. In his book *The Image of the Unseen God* (2017), he offers a very brief consideration of miracles against the backdrop of the qualified process philosophy/theology that he espouses. Hosinski writes,

> The testimony of Christian religious experience, and that of other religious traditions as well, holds that miraculous events do occur. The Gospels present Jesus as one who worked miracles. Even more important, the heart of the Christian gospel proclamation includes the miracle of the resurrection of Jesus from the dead. It does not seem that the Christian tradition can easily give up the claim that miraculous events occur, despite the fact that the intellectual history of the last three centuries in the West has led to even many Christian theologians to "demythologize" or spiritualize such claims, including the claim for the resurrection of Jesus.[9]

At least in principle, Hosinski displays a certain openness to the miraculous. He notes that "in this matter everything depends on how one defines what a miracle is."[10] His interdisciplinary

8. Williams, *Tokens of Trust*, 48.
9. Hosinski, *Image of the Unseen God*, 138.
10. Hosinski, *Image of the Unseen God*, 138.

interest in science and theology leads him to recognize how so much depends on the actual definition of a miracle.

> One of the keys to understanding miracles in a new way resides in the revised understanding of the laws of nature made possible by contemporary science. . . . These laws predict not what must occur, but rather the likelihood or probability of events. . . . With regard to such statistical laws, a miracle may be defined not as a violation of the laws of nature but as an extremely unlikely or improbable event.[11]

There is one important metaphysical consequence of this change of definition—"one can never rule out the possibility of an unlikely or improbable event. So long as that event is not impossible, but is merely highly unlikely, our metaphysics would have to allow for the possibility of its occurrence."[12] Based on the metaphysics of Alfred North Whitehead (1861–1947), Hosinski affirms "the possibility of miracles understood as extremely improbable events." He continues, "If God acts through the presentation of possibilities and lures actual agents toward actualizing the possibility God values most highly, there is no theoretical obstacle to affirming that on occasion God can lure actual agents into actualizing an extremely improbable possibility."[13] He then offers his understanding of the resurrection of Jesus on the basis of this understanding of miracle:

> The resurrection of Jesus from the dead could be understood as an extremely improbable but nevertheless possible objective historical event, not just a subjective event occurring in the hearts and minds of his disciples, as so many theologians have proposed. How exactly the resurrection occurred I cannot suggest, but I would offer the judgment that God elicited life out of an inanimate world once before and I think it not impossible for God to have elicited life out of death in this instance, raising Jesus to

11. Hosinski, *Image of the Unseen God*, 138–39.

12. Hosinski, *Image of the Unseen God*, 139.

13. Hosinski, *Image of the Unseen God*, 139.

> new and transformed life as a promise and revelation of what awaits us all.[14]

Hosinski's position is interesting here. On the one hand, he readily acknowledges the metaphysical improbability of the resurrection of Jesus, and at the same time he notes that epistemologically it cannot be ruled *a priori* as impossible. Constructively, he concludes that the account of the resurrection of Jesus to absolutely new life in God is to be trusted, to be trusted as revealing the Christian hope for the future of everyone.

GABRIEL DALY

In a brief but profound chapter of his book *Asking the Father* (1982), Irish systematic theologian Gabriel Daly (1927–2023) tackles the issue of miracles. The chapter is entitled "The World in Which We Do Our Praying."[15] Primitive human beings did not distinguish between the seen and the unseen worlds, both of which "belonged to the one mysterious theater into which he was born, lived his precarious life, and died."[16] This way of looking at things began to change between 800 BCE and 200 BCE, the period of the higher religions, when human beings began to ask fundamental questions about the meaning of life and reality. This, Daly refers to as the first great revolution in human understanding. The second revolution occurred between the beginning of the sixteenth century and the end of the seventeenth century, introducing a new cosmology with the discoveries made by Copernicus and Galileo. These discoveries challenged the worldview that was informed by Aristotelianism on the one hand and the Bible on the other. A rift developed between the prevailing Christian worldview and the emerging scientific worldview. Daly points out that scientists who were also Christian believers of a sort, like Isaac Newton, tried to effect a reconciliation. Daly summarizes the weaknesses of

14. Hosinski, *Image of the Unseen God*, 140.

15. Daly, *Asking the Father*, 47–65.

16. Daly, *Asking the Father*, 48.

this attempted reconciliation as follows: "With the best will in the world, Newton had created what is today often described as 'the God of the gaps,' i.e., a God who is invoked to fill the provisional and temporary gaps in scientific knowledge. As science filled more and more of these gaps, Newton's God was progressively banished from the universe and was replaced by nature."[17] Thus, phenomena that had traditionally been attributed to God's special intervention in the world could not be explained along scientific lines without recourse to God, and obviously, the reality of the miraculous was called into question. What had appeared as miraculous before was now explicable in terms of science.

Much depends, of course, on how one understands miracle. "The neo-scholastic definition, which prevailed in the Catholic Church before Vatican II, was unequivocal: a miracle is an event which takes place outside, and normally in contradiction of, the course of nature. This definition postulates an intervention of God not merely within the universe he had created but in contravention of the laws he has given it."[18] Seeing God's presence and action in this way, suspending or bypassing the laws of nature, is very problematic. In Daly's terms, "it leaves too many problems unsolved while creating new and gratuitous ones. The sheer inequity, and the seemingly capricious character, of sporadic divine interventions sets up serious questions about the care of God for all his creation. Why are some favored and others not?"[19] Daly points out that the conventionally pious answer to this question is that God knows what is best for each person, and therefore, when to intervene and when not. The image of God that lies behind this conventionally pious response is not very convincing. It smacks of a patronizing and condescending "father knows best" approach to this enormously complex issue.

However, Daly points out that there is an alternative way to approach the issue, and that is to see God's action as "no less present in the processes we understand scientifically than in those

17. Daly, *Asking the Father*, 52.

18. Daly, *Asking the Father*, 55.

19. Daly, *Asking the Father*, 56.

we do not understand. A beautiful sunrise, the smile of a baby, or a Mozart symphony can be miraculous for someone who experiences them in a faith-inspired way. The concept of miracle is a religious not a scientific one."[20] This notion that the concept of miracle is a religious not a scientific concept seems to suggest that miracles are not open to scientific observation and investigation. They are of a different order of truth.

> To the truly believing man or woman any event or phenomenon can be miraculous in that it leads to wonder at the glory and beauty of it all. A miracle thus understood is God's grace lighting up ordinary events in such a way as to provoke wonder or a sense of awe. Whether or not the event or phenomenon can be, either then or later, explained by scientific means is unimportant.[21]

And so, Daly insists, "Paradoxically, it is concern with miracle which may most serve to blind us to God's constant and never failing presence and action in the world."[22]

JOHN MACQUARRIE

The Scottish Anglican theologian John Macquarrie (1919–2007) was one of the most respected and influential English-language theologians of the twentieth century, and not only in his own Anglican Communion. He had a profound influence, for example, on generations of Catholic theologians and seminarians.[23] His approach to theology is both accessible and fairly readily intelligible, not least when it comes to miracles.[24]

"In a minimal sense, a miracle is an event that excites wonder." With this opening remark Macquarrie is referring to the

20. Daly, *Asking the Father*, 56–57.

21. Daly, *Asking the Father*, 57.

22. Daly, *Asking the Father*, 59.

23. For general background, see Cummings, *John Macquarrie*.

24. All references will be to Macquarrie, *Principles of Christian Theology*, 247–53.

linguistic origins of the English word "miracle," that is, to the Latin verb *mirari*, meaning "to wonder, to wonder at." In a religious context, however, there is more to it than simply the excitement of wonder. "It is believed that God is in the event in some special way, that he is the author of it, and intends to achieve some special end by it." In other words a miracle is understood in Christian terms as "an act of God."[25]

In earlier sections of his *Principles of Christian Theology* Macquarrie recognizes that "God is present and active in the whole world-process," and, therefore, "it is clear that some happenings count for more than others, or are more important or significant than others." He does not wish to affirm that somehow everything is miracle, in line with some idealist philosophers and theologians of the nineteenth century, thinkers who were desirous to avoid any notion of sporadic intervention by a God who was outside of the world. He puts it quite succinctly: "Even if all events belong within a continuous series, some stand out within the series as critical moments in its unfolding."[26] To describe every event as somehow miraculous is to evacuate the concept of any genuine meaning.

Equally, Macquarrie does not want to endorse a view of the miraculous as a break in the natural order, a break due to supernatural intervention. He regards such a view as mythological. A modern understanding of science and history makes such an interventionist view of the miraculous incredible. Inevitably, the Christian theologian comes up against "problematic events" that, though well attested, cannot be accounted for in terms of "immanent causal factors."[27] Reports of healings, for example in the New Testament, are a good illustration of such problematic events. Macquarrie regards the healing miracles of the New Testament as more likely and credible than the so-called "nature" miracles. "The reason for our assigning the healing miracles this higher degree of probability is that the same kind of events are reported today from

25. Macquarrie, *Principles*, 247.

26. Macquarrie, *Principles*, 247.

27. For details of an alternative approach to Macquarrie's *Principles*, including a critique of Macquarrie, see Houston, *Reported Miracles*, 83–102.

Lourdes and elsewhere."[28] Macquarrie offers some elucidation—"We simply do not understand how such events happen or what are the intricate linkages." He goes on to comment, "We cannot, in our present state of knowledge concerning nature and man, explain how these events come about." He refuses to see them, however, as "the irruption of a supernatural agency."[29]

He comes to understand a miracle, then, not as something found "in some extraordinary publicly observable event, but in God's presence and self-manifestation in the event. This is not something publicly observable, nor is it something that requires some prodigy, or breach of nature, for its occurrence."[30] The essence of the phenomenon is this *presence and self-manifestation of God.* Since God's acting or presence cannot be proved by publicly observable events, miracle has a certain ambiguous character. "From one point of view, the event is seen as a perfectly ordinary event; from another point of view, it is an event that opens up Being and becomes a vehicle for Being's revelation or grace or judgment or address." Immediately, of course, this raises the question whether a miracle really is being reduced to someone's "subjective apprehension" of it.[31]

As Macquarrie goes further into the matter, he introduces the notion of "focusing." This is what he means by focusing: "God's presence and activity are everywhere and always; yet we experience these intensely in particular concrete happenings, in which, as it were, they have been focused."[32] Again, this raises the question of whether the "subjective apprehension" of miracle is the all-determining factor. Macquarrie, however, recognizes both the objective and the subjective aspects of a miracle. "As revelation is a movement of Being in us, and as symbols are genuinely kin to what they illuminate, so miracle is the approach and self-disclosure of

28. Macquarrie, *Principles*, 249.

29. Macquarrie, *Principles*, 249.

30. Macquarrie, *Principles*, 250.

31. Macquarrie, *Principles*, 250.

32. Macquarrie, *Principles*, 252.

Being to us in and with and through the focusing event, bringing grace or revelation or judgment as the case may be."[33]

The supreme miracle in Christian faith for Macquarrie is the incarnation of our Lord Jesus Christ. This helps a better understanding of this concept of miracle. From one point of view, Jesus was simply another human being. But he was so much more for those who followed him. "But to the disciples, this life was the focusing of the presence and action of God. Faith perceived the dimension which is not publicly observable, and could not be."[34] While faith cannot be proved or disproved simply by observation or argument, in this instance of the incarnation "it is confirmed in the community's subsequent life of faith, where the miracle of incarnation interprets the community's existence, lends meaning to it, strengthens its being."[35] In other words, he suggests that the ongoing, deeper, continually enriched life of the community "confirms" the reality of the miracle of the incarnation. "The sacraments, for instance, are such foci." Through the Eucharist the community finds its life ongoing, deeper, and continually enriched. This is why "talk of the 'miracle of the mass' is not just superstitious talk but points to the focusing of the divine presence of the Eucharist. . . . Miracle is not magic, but the focusing of holy Being's presence and action amid the events, things, and persons of the world, and this has the highest reality."[36]

CONCLUSION

This chapter has outlined the points of view of various respected Christian systematic theologians, from different ecclesial traditions. Two things seem to emerge from their different points of view. First, uniformly all of them reject what might be called an interventionist point of view on God's part with regard to miracles.

33. Macquarrie, *Principles*, 252.

34. Macquarrie, *Principles*, 253.

35. Macquarrie, *Principles*, 253.

36. Macquarrie, *Principles*, 253.

An interventionist point of view seems to suggest that God is normally absent from his creation. All of the above theologians insist on God's presence in and to his creation, his immanence in creation. Second, while there are family resemblances between some of these theologians, they share no universally accepted metaphysics. There is, of course, no revealed metaphysics. In that sense the theologian has to think things through as best he or she can using the best philosophical wisdom available. Inevitably, that means, as can be seen in the above selection, that there will be a plurality of views, and, it must be noted, a plurality of views held by committed Christian theologians.

8

Exploring Moral Evil and Sin with the Novelists Graham Greene and William Styron

Despite what may be, at times, well-founded suspicions, no one really knows the interiority of another. We cannot plumb the depths of another's soul or spirituality without necessarily revealing a great deal about ourselves. Without going into the details of hermeneutical theory, it can be said that any reading of anyone's biography, or any reading of any text that claims our intellectual struggle, is self-involving and is self-revealing, and necessarily so. We do not read with empty heads, nor do we read with empty hearts. Our heads and our hearts, our lives and our experience are, quite simply, full of presuppositions, of interpretations, and of preconceived ideas.

—Owen F. Cummings[1]

We are in fact, each of us, intolerably complex: confused,

1. Cummings, "Grace of Graham Greene," in his *Thinking About Prayer*, 65–66.

bewildered, bombarded by discordant signals and demands, subject to conflictual desires and motives, unstable moods and fragile loyalties; driven by insecurity and ineffectively smothered fear.

—Nicholas Lash[2]

A theodicist who, intentionally or inadvertently, formulates doctrines which occlude the radical and ruthless particularity of human evil is, by implication, mediating a social and political practice which averts its gaze from the cruelties that exist in the world. The theodicist . . . cannot propound views that promote serenity in a heartless world.

—Kenneth Surin[3]

THE MYSTERY OF EVIL/SUFFERING AND THE HUMAN SELF

It is important to distinguish sin from evil. Evil is a much wider term than sin. We might say that evil stands for all of those things we experience in life that we would prefer to avoid—such things as cancer, especially in a small child, earthquakes and tornadoes, floods, famine, etc. While some of these experiences may involve human freedom, most of the time they are simply part of life and creation. We might refer to them as "ontic evil."

On the other hand, sin is the abuse of our human freedom. Freedom is a fundamental constituent of our human nature.

Sin exists when we turn away from the Love that God is, either implicitly or explicitly, as the very center of our life, and we turn in upon the self as the very definition of what is real. This is especially the case when we deal with other human beings no longer as selves who demand our respect and who call forth a loving response but rather as means to our ends, as tools, or as problems.

2. Lash, "On Learning to Be Wise," 358.

3. Surin, *Theology and the Problem of Evil*, 51.

God does not punish human beings for their sins. We do that ourselves. Sin itself provides its own punishment in the distortions and estrangement that it engenders. Loneliness, despair, and entrapment in the futility of the finite cut off from the eternal all serve well as the punishment for sin. God need do nothing.

> Hell is a product of our own misdirected freedom. . . . Every act we perform shapes the self we are. Every act of our freedom has eternal significance, for the self we become is the self we will take into eternity. At the end of life we must present back to God the selves we have become. God will not need to judge us. God will simply put before us the same kind of decisions that we have been facing all our lives.[4]

WHAT ABOUT "ORIGINAL SIN"?

With Tomas Halik

> The terminological pitfalls [of talking about original sin] were highlighted by Karl Rahner . . . when he opened his exposition of the dogma of original sin by saying that it was first necessary to realize that it was neither "original"—that is, something unique to be transmitted—nor a "sin" in the way that the term is generally understood. The "original sin" is not something "inherited" in a biological or genetic sense; the word "sin" in this case does not indicate some single "immoral act," but a state in which human existence finds itself.[5]

And Edward Yarnold, SJ

> No man is an island. We are not individuals who happen to have relations with others; our relations with others

4. Raschko, *Christian Understanding of Human Nature*, 175–76.
5. Halik, *Night of the Confessor*, 85.

> constitute what we are. We find ourselves in a selfish, divided society, and inevitably ourselves become selfish and out of harmony with our fellows.[6]

And Joseph Ratzinger

> The account [in the Book of Genesis] tells us that sin begets sin, and that, therefore, all the sins of history are interlinked. Theology refers to this state of affairs by the certainly misleading and imprecise term "original sin." . . . At the very moment that a person begins human existence, which is a good, he or she is confronted by a sin-damaged world. Each of us enters into a situation in which relationality has been hurt. Consequently each person is, from the very start, damaged in relationships and does not engage in them as he or she ought. Sin pursues the human being, and he or she capitulates to it.[7]

READING FROM TWO NOVELISTS, REFLECTING ON "SIN"

> I am afraid of people who never read novels, because they tend to be people who seem the most unwilling . . . to suspend disbelief and to risk entering into another's world where you are never quite sure if you are hearing the truth or being offered counterfeit currency.
>
> David Jasper[8]

Graham Greene, *The Heart of the Matter*

Graham Greene's novel *The Heart of the Matter* (1948) concerns several months in the life of Major Henry Scobie. Scobie is a

6. Yarnold, *Theology of Original Sin*, 76.
7. Ratzinger, "'*In the beginning* . . .,'" 72–73.
8. Jasper, "Echoes of Laughter," 414.

complicated man and the character arguably reflects something of Graham Greene's own complexity. After fifteen years of colonial service in Sierra Leone, Scobie is, for all practical purposes, broken by the circumstances of his life. The Second World War is on, and his posting is in a relatively insignificant British colony. At forty-nine, he is the assistant commissioner of police. His only child is dead, and he is unable to communicate with his wife, Louise, whom he no longer loves. She has become somewhat neurotic after the death of their child, and Scobie feels for her something akin to pity and responsibility. He overhears her referred to as "literary Louise," because of her interest in poetry and literature, and is offended by the remark. An acquaintance says of the Scobies' marriage and in reference to a rumor of the major's infidelity, "Perhaps if I had a wife like that, I'd sleep with niggers too." In actual fact, there is no basis for Scobie's infidelity other than some degree of openness to the Africans not widely shared in colonial circles.

There are additional difficulties. The Scobies have been slighted: Scobie has been passed over for promotion, and Louise is not pleased. Her displeasure has been all too accurately summarized in this way: "In the small, spitefully intimate colonial society, Louise feels the slight keenly, and vents her spleen on the long-suffering Scobie." She would like to go to South Africa for a vacation to get away from it all, but there is a problem with money. Scobie approaches his local bank manager for a loan but is turned down, and this leads him to dealing with the dishonest Syrian trader Yusef.

At the end of Book One, Scobie has obtained the money he needs from Yusef, and so Louise is off for her vacation. At the beginning of Book Two, Scobie is receiving survivors from a torpedoed ship off the coast of Sierra Leone, and visits the hospital where the survivors are recovering. He gives comfort to a dying child in her last moments by making the shadow of a rabbit's head on the wall with his hands; Scobie even prays for the little girl: "Father . . . give her peace. Take away my peace forever, but give her peace." The dying child says, "Father," thinking Scobie be her dead father. He remains with the child until she dies: "Yes, dear.

Don't speak. I'm here." He also meets in the hospital Helen Rolt, a nineteen-year-old woman and now a widow after only one month of marriage—her husband had died in the open boat in which she survived after their ship was torpedoed. Scobie helps Helen, who becomes both his friend and his lover.

After a quarrel with Helen, Scobie writes a letter to her protesting his love for her, but the letter is intercepted by a servant of the unscrupulous trader Yusef, who then uses the letter to blackmail Scobie into diamond smuggling. In this intercepted and never-received letter, Scobie had written, "I love you more than myself, more than my wife, more than God I think."

In Book Three, Louise returns from her South African vacation. She is resigned to Scobie's failure to achieve promotion but she now sees it as her mission in life to be the custodian of his religious duties and observance as a Catholic. She wants him to receive Holy Communion with her. Scobie, as a Catholic, cannot go to the sacrament without first receiving forgiveness in the sacrament of confession and penance for his sin of adultery. His confessor, the Catholic priest Father Rank, refuses forgiveness to him because there is no firm purpose of amendment on Scobie's part because Scobie refuses to give up Helen. He needs, however, to keep up appearances for his own sake, as faithful husband, and as a faithful lover. He approaches the sacrament:

> Father Rank came down the steps from the altar bearing the Host. The saliva had dried in Scobie's mouth: it was as though his veins had dried. He couldn't look up; he saw only the priest's skirt like the skirt of the medieval warhorse bearing down upon him: the flapping of feet: the charge of God. . . . But with open mouth (the time had come) he made one last attempt at prayer, "O God, I offer up my damnation to you. Take it. Use it for them," and he was aware of the pale papery taste of an eternal sentence on the tongue.

In his own eyes Scobie was damning himself, but doing so in order to defend the two women he judged to be helpless without him. In a subsequent conversation with Helen, when he tells her that he has condemned himself to hell in receiving the Eucharist unworthily, she accuses him of having done so not out of love for her but because he was afraid that Louise would find out about their affair. Scobie responds, "Love for both of you. If it were just for her, there would be an easy straight way." He put his hands over his eyes, feeling hysteria beginning to mount again. He said, "I can't bear to see suffering, and I cause it all the time. I want to get out, get out."

As if to confirm his own self-condemnation during this moral and spiritual malaise, and as he is about to deliver contraband diamonds, Scobie foolishly distrusts his loyal servant Ali. In a drunken state he shares with Yusef his doubts about Ali's trustworthiness, doubts that are utterly without any foundation in fact, and Yusef assures Scobie that he will take care of Ali for him. This he does by having the man murdered. Scobie finds Ali's body, and he sees it as "like a broken piece of the rosary . . . a couple of black beads and the image of God coiled at the end of it. O God, he thought, I've killed you: you've served me all these years and I've killed you at the end of them. God lay there under the petrol drums."

There is no more hope left in Scobie's sad life. For the sake of Louise he plans a suicide that will look like natural death so that Louise will get the life-insurance money. He pretends to have angina, stockpiles the regular doses of medicine, and prepares to overdose. Shortly before doing so, however, he learns that the job for which he had been passed over will now be his, that is, commissioner of police. After being told that he is the man for the job, Scobie thinks,

> "So all this need not have happened. If Louise had stayed, I should never have loved Helen, I would never have been blackmailed by Yusef, never committed that act of despair. I would have been myself still . . . ." But, of course, he told himself it's only because I have done these things that success comes. I am of the devil's party. He looks after his own in this world. I shall go now from damned success to damned success, he thought with disgust.

After taking the overdose of medication, Greene describes Scobie's last words and his death. He said aloud, "'Dear God, I love . . .,' but the effort was too great and he did not feel his body when it struck the floor." Who is it Scobie loves? "Dear God. I love . . ." One can make a case for Louise, for Helen, for Ali. One can make a case for God. Personally, I think a case can be made for loving the Love that God is, and for others in and through and with that God, not outside God.

Louise finally goes to see Father Rank. She needs to speak to him about her husband, his suicide, and his adultery. She is hurt and wounded and in need of deep healing. She tells Rank that Scobie was "a bad Catholic." The priest responds, "That's the silliest phrase in common use." Louise goes on to say to the priest that there is no point in praying for her suicidal husband, because suicide puts one beyond the pale of God's mercy and love. Such prayer is an absolute waste of time. Father Rank replies,

> "For goodness' sake, Mrs. Scobie, don't imagine you or I know a thing about God's mercy." "The church says . . .," she interrupts. "I know what the church says," Rank responds. "The church knows all the rules. But it doesn't know what goes on in a single human heart."

Commentary

What are we to make of the fictional but all too real Henry Scobie? Suffering is all around him and he has been both the cause and the effect of suffering. Has Henry Scobie done bad things, has he made poor moral choices, has he sinned? I think the answer has to be "Yes," but at the same time a *qualified* "Yes." Think of his circumstances: the complexity of war, the horrendous loss of a child, the consequent loveless marriage, the humiliation at once personal and social of being passed over for promotion, the financial inability to ameliorate the situation, just to state the beginnings of Scobie's fall.

Has Henry Scobie fallen from grace? I want to fall back on the sentiments of Father Rank, especially Father Rank's words, "[The church] doesn't know what goes on in a single human heart." The church is undoubtedly the premier sacrament of salvation, as in Vatican II's *Lumen Gentium* par. 1, but it would be blasphemous rationalism to think that the church defines God's grace, God's salvation. I think that loving trust is to be found in Scobie, even in the complex ambiguity of his sinfulness.

While Henry Scobie takes his own life, another fictional contemporary, Jemand von Niemand, takes the lives of others in *Sophie's Choice*.

William Styron, *Sophie's Choice*

> *To stand in Auschwitz is to have your backbone turned into a question mark about the nature of human being.*
>
> John Moriarty[9]

William Styron's novel *Sophie's Choice* (1979) contains an account of a man, Jemand von Niemand, who sought to reconcile himself to God by bringing himself to commit a most evil deed.[10] Sophie Zawistowska, the "heroine" of the novel, was arrested in Poland during the Second World War and has been deported to Auschwitz along with her children Jan and Eva. Arriving at Auschwitz railway station, they are faced with the dreaded selection procedure, some to be consigned immediately to the gas chambers, others to slavery. The selection is conducted by the SS doctor, Jemand von Niemand:

> "Are you Polish," said the doctor. "Are you also a communist." . . . [Instead] of keeping her mouth shut Sophie said, "I am Polish! I was born in Krakow!" Then she blurted helplessly, "I'm not Jewish! Or my children—they're not

9. John Moriarty (1938–2007) was an Irish philosopher and author. This unacknowledged quotation is taken from Gallagher, *Human Poetry of Faith*, 30.

10. See also the interesting essay by Surin, "Atonement and Moral Apocalyticism."

Jewish either." And she added, "They are racially pure. They speak German." Finally she announced, "I'm a Christian. I'm a devout Catholic."

She heard Dr. von Niemand say, "So you're not a communist. You're a believer." "Yes. I believe in Christ" . . .

"So you believe in Christ the Redeemer?" the doctor said. . . . "Did Christ not say, 'Suffer the little children to come unto me?'" He turned back to her, with the twitchy methodicalness of a drunk. Sophie was about to attempt to reply when the doctor said, "You may keep one of your children."

"What!" said Sophie. "You may keep one of your children," he repeated. "The other one will have to go. Which one will you keep?"

Her thought processes dwindled, ceased. Then she felt her legs crumble. "I can't choose! I can't choose!" She began to scream. . . . The doctor was aware of unwanted attention. "Shut up!" he ordered. "Hurry now and choose. Choose, God dammit, or I'll send them both over there. Quick!"

"Don't make me choose," she heard herself plead in a whisper, "I can't choose."

"Send them both over there, then," the doctor said to the aide.

"Mama!" She heard Eva's cry at the instant that she thrust the child away from her and rose from the concrete with a clumsy stumbling motion. "Take the baby!" she called out, "Take my little girl!"

At this point the aide—with a careful gentleness that Sophie would try without success to forget—tugged at Eva's hand and led her away into the waiting legion of the damned. She would forever retain a dim impression that the child had continued to look, beseeching.

Later Sophie found out from one of the other inmates of the camp, who knew the doctor from her youth in Berlin, that Dr. von Niemand was "a steadfast churchgoer and that he had always planned to enter the ministry. A mercenary father forced him into medicine."

Commentary

This, then, is Sophie's choice. Words are totally inadequate to the task of representing to us the truth of the unspeakable darkness and shame of von Niemand's deed. The nature of this deed is such that it begs us to affirm the hard words of Professor Ulrich Simon (whose father perished in Auschwitz): "I do not myself believe that there can be forgiveness for Auschwitz. . . . Not only the monstrosity, but also the impersonal 'nothingness' of the evil render this remission immoral and impossible." Any attempt rationally to comprehend the enormity of what went on in Auschwitz is bound to be futile—as George Steiner points out, the world of the extermination camps is a world that is "extraterritorial to reason."[11]

And the von Niemands of this world? Let me offer an opinion. The church talks about our "immortal souls," but really "immortality" belongs to God alone. The language about immortal souls is a way of describing how much God loves us, how special each of us is to him, as he offers his love to us to be in union, in communion with him. Love cannot be coerced, only offered. The direction of our moral lives is our response to the offer. When we refuse to respond in love to Love, through our responses to God's creation and especially to his human creatures, we literally lose something of ourselves, we lose something of our "souls." The immense enormity of the loss is exemplified in von Niemand. He has extinguished himself, he has annihilated his soul. He has chosen to be "nothing," the literal meaning of the name *Niemand*. That is what I think Ulrich Simon means when he says that there cannot be forgiveness for Auschwitz. It cannot mean, it seems to me, that there is ever a lack of forgiving love on God's part. But the loving response of the human heart is absolutely required for that final loving communion with God. Not to respond with love to Love is to choose to be nothing, *Niemand*.

However, having read Ulrich Simon's *Theology of Auschwitz* (1967), I cannot leave it there. Simon points out in the book that

11. Ulrich Simon and George Steiner quoted in Surin, "Atonement and Moral Apocalypticism," 104.

Auschwitz not only brought out the worst in people, as in the case of the fictional yet all too real von Niemand, but also the best. The best? Not only the well-known names of the Catholics Maximilian Kolbe (1894–1941), Edith Stein (1891–1942), murdered at Auschwitz, but also the Jewess Etty Hillesum (1914–43), and, in a different way and in the concentration camp of Flossenburg, Dietrich Bonhoeffer (1906–45). Their kindness, generosity, and compassionate witness are exemplary. Ulrich Simon also points out the numerous and anonymous "little people," as it were, condemned to be murdered and to be incinerated who daily helped one another.

Simon goes on to say this: "A theology of Auschwitz cannot be written unless its findings issue in prayer, for we can face the horror only by coming to terms with it liturgically."[12] This could be interpreted in a negative fashion, of course, as evasive of the horror of the Shoah. But I think that finally, ultimately, eschatologically, only praise "works," the praise of the unfathomable Loving God. Praise-prayer-worship seems to me to be the only ecology within which to live without totalizing despair.

TURNING TO WORDS OF THEOLOGIAN DAVID FORD

As we conclude this chapter I want to turn to some words of theologian David Ford:

> Then there is the other side of being hurt which is often inseparable from it: hurting others. The wisdom of the religions is clear: by hurting others we wound our own heart more terribly than by anything others can inflict on us. This is almost unimaginable, to think that being nasty to someone is worse for us than suffering them being nasty to us. It is not true that the worst thing that can happen to us is being wronged, wounded, or even killed: the worst thing is to do wrong. The double tragedy is that

12. Simon, *Theology of Auschwitz*, 47.

> our wounds, which can be so terrible, are often an almost irresistible temptation to inflict wounds on others.[13]

While exploring moral evil through fiction—through characters like Scobie and von Niemand—yields some insight, it is not enough until we focus exploration on ourselves. That is the importance of Ford's observation. Christians need to look into their own hearts, preferably on a daily basis, to search out what traces of evil—in Ford's words "hurting others"—are lurking there. We are not immune from the banality of evil, to use the phrase of Hannah Arendt.[14] Fundamental to what Arendt means by banality is the human propensity for not thinking, not thinking through the full remit of our words and actions. That is why it is so necessary to examine oneself daily. In the church's Liturgy of the Hours, the office of Compline at the end of the day offers an opportunity for the examination of conscience. Ultimately, we cannot pass judgment on Scobie and von Niemand without this regular *self*-examination.

13. Ford, *Shape of Living*, 14.

14. Arendt, *Eichmann in Jerusalem*.

9

Narrative Theological Approaches to Evil and Suffering

Diamonds of wisdom-through-suffering have been produced under the most intense pressures, and if we find one, it is to be treasured. . . . Those who go through their suffering and produce (or even, in a sense become) a diamond that can reflect the light of hope, are offering other people the most precious gift imaginable.

—David F. Ford[1]

INTRODUCTION

These words of theologian David Ford are absolutely right. People who have gone through intense suffering and yet remained hopeful are wonderful witnesses, and are to be treasured. The saints commemorated throughout the liturgical year are often such a treasure. We find their names in the Litany of Saints, for example, in the celebration of baptism, and most especially at the Easter Vigil. At the same time, there are so many other Christians not

1. Ford, *Shape of Living*, 166.

so well known who are, in Ford's words, "diamonds-of-wisdom-through-suffering," and it is to these witnesses that I now wish to turn.

FRANCES M. YOUNG

Frances Young (1939–) is a Methodist biblical and patristic theologian. Looking back on a life complicated and made extremely difficult by caring at home for her severely handicapped son Arthur (born in 1967), severely brain damaged and unable to learn to do anything for himself, she writes, "I could only look back on all that had happened with a sense of gratitude and an awareness of the grace of providence. Somehow God seemed behind and before everything."[2] That is a remarkable statement. For decades Frances and her husband Bob looked after Arthur, tending to all his needs even as they both worked, Frances as a theologian and Bob as a scientist. Her fundamental conviction was of God's gracious presence "behind and before everything." This is how she puts it: "There has been no easy triumph, but the pain is shot through with joy, and the joy is pierced with pain."[3] As a colleague of John Hick's in the Department of Theology of the University of Birmingham, she was fully aware of Hick's approach to the issue of evil and suffering. When discussing John Hick's view of the universe as a place of soul-making—in our terms, a prospective view of suffering—she has this to say:

> If God's purpose was "soul-making," what about a new human being without the potential to respond and grow and mature in faith and in virtue? Even if I could allow that there was something good in my relationship with Arthur, that he was a trigger for deeper love, he represented the cases where there is no potential, the cases where handicap does not produce greater love but the kind of desperate burden that causes a marriage to crack, distorts the development of other children, and leads to

2. Young, *Face to Face*, 3.

3. Young, *Face to Face*, 50.

> family breakdown. I began to see clearly the profound ambiguity of suffering and its power to discriminate, to bring out the best and bring out the worst in people.[4]

She understood experientially the difficult ambiguities that come with suffering. No attempt was made to glide over the facts or to escape from them.

In the midst of her work as a Christian theologian and caring for Arthur, Frances Young underwent a powerful sense of vocation.

> In fact, it was the sense of vocation which changed me. . . . I was quite overwhelmed by the sense that God had loved me all along, and somehow everything in my life fell into place. . . . Above all I felt extraordinary exultation. It was sheer amazement that one who had so little deserved it had been brought through such a wilderness of desolation and loneliness, and had never in fact been left alone, but always loved and guided. . . . My own experience is of a transfiguring something like that which is often expressed in love poems. The ordinary world requires an extraordinary dimension. . . . Indeed, it has been just like falling in love all over again. . . . As far as I am concerned, on the one hand God transcends all anthropomorphic idols—he is a mystery, beyond the personal; on the other hand, I know him in a relationship to which the relationship with my husband is the closest analogy—that remarkable sense of trust and mutual commitment, that inability to imagine life without him, and moments of inexpressible joy.[5]

Her sense of vocation and the commitments of every day over time strengthened in her. She is able to say,

> But I do know that we are in the hands of God, and nothing else matters. . . . In God's presence the demand for explanation ceases. God is sufficient in himself to bring a perspective which transcends and transforms. That is

4. Young, *Face to Face*, 58.
5. Young, *Face to Face*, 85–88.

> more or less my experience. Face to face with God, the problems do not disappear but they do appear different.[6]

I'm not sure that "in God's presence the demand for explanation ceases." As reasonable beings seeking to understand our Christian faith, we shall probably continue to seek for explanation. That's the lot of being human. However, when she affirms that face to face with God "the problems do not disappear but they do appear different," that insight is full of wisdom, implicitly acknowledging that God is nothing but Love, even in darkness.

MARGARET SPUFFORD

British journalist Andrew Brown says this of historian Margaret Spufford (1935–2014):

> She was more ill, more often, than anyone I have known. As a young woman her studies at both Oxford and Cambridge had been interrupted by breakdowns. In her 30s she was crippled by early onset osteoporosis, followed by cancer and heart disease; finally the indignities and inadequacies consequent from a series of strokes brought her slowly to a place where she was immobile and almost speechless, unable even to swallow, though she still could laugh. . . . For someone who had talked as much and as wonderfully as she did, this was terrible. What made it more terrible was the knowledge that it was love that kept her alive, and so love that made all that suffering possible. It was the love of her family and of her friends—she would have said the love of God through them—that gave her the reasons for living, and so for suffering.[7]

As well as her own health struggles, Margaret struggled with the sufferings of her daughter Bridget, who was born with the metabolic disease cystinosis. Bridget was in and out of hospital all her life. The Spuffords were a family marked by great tragedy.

6. Young, *Face to Face*, 89–92.

7. Andrew Brown in his obituary of Margaret Spufford in the British newspaper *The Guardian*, March 20, 2014.

In 1992 Margaret published a most moving narrative of suffering with the title *Celebration*. Here is Margaret's own account of how she coped with suffering:

> At first sight a book which is about physical or mental pain may seem very oddly titled *Celebration*. But it is written by a woman to whom, over the years, participation in the Eucharist has become the most important part of living and being in silence before the reserved sacrament the most important part of prayer. Gradually, and with immense diffidence, I have come to see that my own participation in this offering of the Eucharist must involve the presentation of my own experience, for hallowing, along with "the best bread that can conveniently be gotten," in the hope that it, too, can be redeemed and transformed.[8]

We notice several things in this passage. First, the Eucharist has become "the most important part of living." I think many Christians would want to ally themselves with this point of view, even as they might find it very difficult to do so. Second, as she participates in the Eucharist, she does so in hope that her own experience of suffering will be "redeemed and transformed." As the bread and wine are transformed by God into the very presence of Christ, his body and blood, Margaret's hope is for a similar transformation of her suffering. Her words remind me of Benedict of Canfield's perspective on suffering mentioned in chapter 7—reverencing our suffering as the suffering of Christ, not just passively but also in the hope of resurrection-transformation. Third, she speaks of "living and being in silence before the reserved sacrament [as] the most important part of prayer." This is, of course, a most personal experience for her, but if we think of the reserved sacrament as the prolonged expression of Christ's eucharistic presence, it makes so much sense. Later in the book Margaret continues to comment on her eucharistic experience:

> The center of this pain, and also of this silence and light, lies in the Eucharist. Sometimes we are ill-served by

8. Spufford, *Celebration*, 20.

> familiarity. Even the language of the original events that we re-enact, Eucharist by Eucharist, has become so familiar to us that it has lost some of its force, partly through constant repetition. From the phraseology of picking up our cross, and following our Lord, we have to strip all the clothing of habit, take it back to its original meaning, and think of his torture and of his death on a gibbet. Sometimes I cannot understand our external placidity, as we stand there, faced now, afresh, with the agony of this death, and the flies on these wounds. The reenactment is a burning-glass, focusing pain, drawing together all those screams I have heard, all those broken branches and bruised flowers, all those fossils in the Grand Canyon, all the fears I have for my own future of cumulative fracture. There is nothing, ultimately, nothing, that I can do of myself to transform all this pain. There have been times I wanted to scream . . . and I have not been able to bear to go at all. I do remember how once my own pain was transformed for me by pure gift, by the presence of the Crucified. . . . But it is because the celebration of the Eucharist and Christ's offering of himself in it seems to comprehend all the realities of acute pain and death that I have not handed in my ticket. . . . There is a completeness to adoration: the soul is stilled in the presence of God, there is nothing left to desire.[9]

This is a remarkable paragraph. She acknowledges her desire at times to scream at all this brutal suffering. But the presence of Christ in which she participates sacramentally comes to her as "pure gift" enabling her to continue and to give up in understandable despair or hopelessness.

Margaret writes of Bridget's death most movingly:

> Two days after I returned home after writing this book, our daughter [Bridget] became ill with what was eventually diagnosed as a neurological failure. . . . Her decline was in no sense amusing. However, she was given the gift of clarity and serenity in the last month of her life and was precisely aware of what was happening and to

9. Spufford, *Celebration*, 86–90.

> Whom she was going. It was a month which all four of us [Bridget, Margaret, her husband and son] were mainly able to spend in her bedroom at home, reading aloud, listening to music, and surrounded by flowers. She died in all our arms, very soon after her 22nd birthday on the Sunday after Ascension Day, 1989.[10]

KATHRYN GREENE-MCCREIGHT

Kathryn Greene-McCreight (1961–) is included in these narrative theological approaches to evil and suffering primarily because she has the great courage to speak openly about her mental health challenges. Kathryn has a doctorate in theology from Yale University and serves as an Anglican priest in Connecticut. Writing in 2006, she says, "I have struggled with clinical mental illness for the last quarter of my life," a diagnosis "as manic and therefore bipolar disorder," bouncing "between depression and mania."[11] She tells us what she hopes to do in her book:

> I do not intend to search out and ground philosophical consistency for "solving" the problem of evil; I am no philosopher. I am concerned instead to offer a biblically grounded account, from my own experience, of how the Christian may interpret, accept, and handle suffering, especially that with such a stigma as mental illness.[12]

She found support and comfort through love and through prayer as she faced the onset of her mental illness beginning in 1992. Her husband's unfailing love was a constant support. This is how she describes it:

> Human loves, such as that of my husband, can certainly be a conduit for divine love, even for those who do not recognize love's true source. If it is the love of God that we see in the face of Christ Jesus that is promised to pull

10. Spufford, *Celebration*, 123.
11. Greene-McCreight, *Darkness*, 11.
12. Greene-McCreight, *Darkness*, 12.

> us through, a love that bears out to the edge of doom even for the ugly and unlovable such as we, then the statement that love heals depression is in fact the only light that exists in the dark tunnel.[13]

I'm sure many can identify with her words here. They reflect the sentiment of St. Paul in 1 Corinthians 13:8–13: "Love is patient and kind. . . . Love never fails." (I prefer the translation of verse 8 as "Love never fails"—the Greek verb is *piptō*, to fall—over the more usual "Love never ends" because it seems to me not only more concrete but also more dynamic.) In slightly different language, Kathryn, I believe, is affirming that human love is a sacrament of Divine Love. Later in the book she speaks of her husband's love with intimacy:

> My husband, Matthew, just wants to help. He keeps asking me what he can do. He says that he feels so helpless. He is helpless, and so am I. There is nothing he can do. Yet maybe there is. I tell him not to treat me like an invalid. When I can't get up, when I can't crack a smile through my plaster mask of a face, when I can't do anything but weep, just hold my hand. *But please don't be in pain for me.* Because then I can see that on your face, and it makes my pain worse. Just treat me in a matter-of-fact way: Kathryn is depressed again. Or when I am manic, don't get scared of me. Don't get mad at me just because I talk too much, have too much energy, burst at the seams with ideas for the garden, the house, vacations, books. It is not my fault that I swing from one extreme to the other: I know loving me right now is a big challenge. But that's how I can be helped.[14]

She also underscores the importance of prayer, alongside, of course, appropriate drugs and therapy/counseling:

> The assurance that people were praying for me, since I had so much trouble praying for myself, was a salve. My true friends during this time were the ones I knew were

13. Greene-McCreight, *Darkness*, 24.

14. Greene-McCreight, *Darkness*, 73.

> praying for me. . . . I do not mean to say that the *idea* of people praying for me was a great comfort, although I do suppose this is true to an extent. I mean the *fact* that people were praying for me was key in my dealing with my illness.[15]

Kathryn shares with Margaret Spufford the faith-conviction that our suffering is a participation in the sufferings of Christ, and not, as it were, just something to put up with.

> For the Christian, who believes in the crucified and risen Messiah, suffering is always meaningful. It is meaningful because of the One in whose suffering we participate, Jesus. This is neither to say, of course, that suffering will be pleasant nor that it is to be sought. Rather, the personal suffering of the Christian finds a correlate in Christ's suffering, which gathers up our tears, calms our sorrows, and points us toward his resurrection.[16]

This the mystical vision of the cross discussed in chapter 7. Notice too the important point she makes—suffering is not to be sought out for its own sake. This is the heart of Kathryn's story. At the same time, she goes on in the book to offer sound guidance about how to deal with mental illness.

DANIEL W. HARDY

Daniel Hardy (1930–2007) was the director of the Princeton Center of Theological Inquiry, before which he had been Van Mildert Professor of Theology in the University of Durham, and before that senior lecturer in theology at the University of Birmingham. He and his wife retired to Cambridge, England, where Deborah (Dan's daughter) and David Ford (Dan's son-in-law) and their family were living and working. Unlike our other examples, Dan did not experience a lifetime of suffering. When he was given six months to live, he began a series of conversations with his daughter and

15. Greene-McCreight *Darkness*, 35.
16. Greene-McCreight, *Darkness*, 37.

son-in-law, and with a Jewish theologian with whom he had been working over the years, Peter Ochs. They became his interlocutors in these last six months, helping to put together a series of reflections that constitute the book entitled *Wording a Radiance* (2010).

Dan was a systematic theologian, and his thought is both rigorous and analytic, and also deeply insightful. Just before the preface to *Wording a Radiance* he has this to say:

> I've been content ever since the onset of this cancer to be drawn into death, but I don't take this negatively at all: it is also being drawn into life and the two are closely tied together. . . . I don't know how: being drawn into death is also being drawn into life. . . . Perhaps I am being a sort of sign of attraction, going ahead of you into the mystery, an attraction not into anything clear and unambiguous but into a light that is the mystery of death and life, and therein God. This is about my almost insatiable concern for God, not just for knowledge about God but a more insatiable thirst again than that. . . . It is a question of allowing the divine to flood in without inhibition.[17]

I knew Dan when I was teaching theology in Birmingham in the early 1980s, and I can hear his voice behind these faith-filled words. Some of the words stand out. "Going ahead of you into the mystery . . . and therein God." His Christian faith is clear, but he realizes that our journey into God as we leave this world is marked by a certain ambiguity. The Christian tradition does not possess an ordnance survey map of the last things, as it were, but nonetheless faith stands firm. I appreciate especially his "almost insatiable concern for God," and "allowing the divine to flood in without inhibition." The words are so carefully chosen. Anyone who knew him would testify to Dan's insatiable concern for God. Dan was a priest in the Anglican Communion and so he celebrated the Eucharist and preached regularly. His insatiable concern was not simply intellectual, although it was that. He was possessed by a passionate pastoral concern to communicate God to others. We see this in his words "allowing the divine to flood in without inhibition," a

17. This is from the unnumbered page immediately before the preface.

beautiful description of Christian life and particularly the life of a theologian.

As the book proceeds, he comments further on the centrality of God-flooding-in:

> The world should be translucent to the divine: that's what I hope for, but the world does not show itself as it was divinely originated. So I am disappointed when it doesn't. . . . I am disappointed in the world when it gets formerly caught up in its extensity—its sheer spread out-ness—and becomes confused and chaotic. . . . My whole life and work has been an ecclesiological response to the malaise of extensity. The intensity I seek has a maternal dimension. I seek maternal being in ideas: a light attracting me with its warmth. God has maternal intensity, which extensity does not provide.[18]

Dan yearned that the world "should be translucent to the divine." This is really a mystical yearning, to recognize and to respond to the world filled with God.

> [The light of God] heals without overburdening; that's not in its nature. Christians often want a strong right arm. They talk in the language of power, but that's not what it's about; it's about a gentle infiltration from within, not coming at you from outside, like a ton of bricks. How does light happen within the world? It irradiates from within. It's like seeing people "light up" within; it's a huge privilege, and we have to recognize and discern it in one another and to embrace and delight in it.[19]

With very little time left, the book reproduces some of the conversations between Dan and his daughter Deborah, also an Anglican priest.

> He was not frightened of his tumor or of dying. He even found it very difficult when searching letters arrived saying "We're praying for a miracle." He said it wasn't right—"How can we expect to be excused from our

18. Hardy et al., *Wording a Radiance*, 23.
19. Hardy et al., *Wording a Radiance*, 35–36.

humanity?" He saw cancer and suffering as "normality" in the world as it is now—that "tumors happen and need to be received." And he believed strongly that it was part of the priestly vocation to teach and show people how to die well. [Deborah] asked, "How do you reconcile the fact that you want to live and fight the tumor for as long as possible, and being peaceful and ready to die when the time comes?" "You can't reconcile them," was his reply. "The task is to be open and available to be used by God for as long as he wants."[20]

[Deborah] had a new sense of urgency: "I don't know how much longer we have left together, Dad. Would you like me to anoint you?" "Yes I would, I'd like that very much," he said; and (with a smile), "I need all the help I can get!" "I wonder what it is going to be like (dying)?" [Deborah] wondered. And he answered very calmly: "It's just going to happen, bit by bit: it's a matter of going with it." From that moment I handed over my priestly role: we now needed to be simply "father and daughter" again and be ministered to as such. We later (following the administration of the last rites) celebrated Communion together as a family and were all hugely relieved at the end when the priest said, "Well, that's the formal good-bye—but now you hold on to him for as long as you can." Later that evening, having already said good night to my father, I went back again: "Just in case anything happens tonight Dad, you know how much I love you, don't you?" He answered: "I love you too. Double. Complete." These were the last words he spoke to me: words of praise, just as he had hoped. . . . The whole family was gathered—surrounding him with the "ordinariness" of life and love that was also very special—and for the first time there was the sense that somehow "all would be well." Along with them later, I said, "It's okay, Dad; we're going to be all right. You can let go when you need to."[21]

20. Hardy et al., *Wording a Radiance*, 140.

21. Hardy et al., *Wording a Radiance*, 148–49.

CONCLUSION

Many could find undoubtedly "diamonds-of-wisdom-through-suffering" among family members, friends, and acquaintances. I have chosen these four because I found that they spoke to me in a very special way. Frances Young and Daniel Hardy I knew personally. I don't recall who introduced me to Margaret Spufford, but I was immediately taken by her book *Celebration*. Members of my family have suffered with mental-health challenges and when I came across the work of Kathryn Greene-McCreight, I came to a better understanding of the phenomenon. What is really important for me through these four diamonds is their vibrant Christian faith. We are often told that faith comes by hearing and that is surely true. Faith comes to us a gift from God mediated through others. Faith also comes from reading, from reading real life-stories, and that is why I have entitled this chapter "narrative theological approaches to evil and suffering."

10

Death and God's Lovely Presence

Emily Dickinson, John Henry Newman, Kallistos Ware

Death, and our attitude towards it, lies at the heart of the problem of suffering; it issues the supreme challenge to the virtue of hope.

—James Walsh and P. G. Walsh[1]

THE MYSTERY OF DEATH WITH EMILY DICKINSON

There is much merit in considering what the Catholic Church teaches about eschatology.[2] However, in this chapter, I want to turn to poetry for theological insight, and first to the American poet Emily Dickinson (1830–86). Dickinson was not especially well

1. Walsh and Walsh, *Divine Providence and Human Suffering*, 180.

2. For those who wish to pursue this route, I recommend Dermot A. Lane's *Keeping Hope Alive* (1996) and Robin Ryan's *Life Is Changed, Not Ended* (2024), both of which are excellent introductions to contemporary discussions.

known in her lifetime. She was, however, unusually insightful and can offer us new perspectives on death.

Because I could not stop for Death
He kindly stopped for me.
The Carriage held but just Ourselves—
And Immortality.[3]

In the poem, death is understood as a gentleman stopping his carriage so that the speaker—Emily herself in this case—could step into his carriage. The adverb "kindly" strongly suggests a certain courteous aspect of personified Death. While the speaker and Death are in the carriage—"just ourselves"—immortality is also there. The inevitability and seeming finality of death are accompanied by immortality or the gift of eternal life. It would seem in the poem that death is better understood not as an enemy to be feared so much as a courteous accompaniment of the living, eventually leading to eternal life.

Another poem from Emily Dickinson, "My Life Closed Twice Before Its Close" (c. 1852) goes like this:

My life closed twice before its close;
It yet remains to see
If Immortality unveil
A third event to me,
So huge, so hopeless to conceive,
As these that twice befell.
Parting is all we know of heaven,
And all we need of hell.[4]

Dickinson is describing her grief over losing two people she loved in life. Her grief is so overwhelming, "so huge, so hopeless to conceive," that it felt like death itself. That leads her to affirm the famous couplet: "Parting is all we know of heaven, and all we need of hell." In that sense she is absolutely right. Parting from those we love in death is what we know for certain about heaven, and parting from hell is all we need to know about hell. The teachings of the

3. Dickinson, *Poems of Emily Dickinson*, poem no. 479.

4. The poem is in the public domain.

church about the "last things" are but commentary on these two affirmations. The church does not provide us with an ordnance survey map of what happens after death, but rather the slimmest of outlines. Dickinson's contemporary John Henry Newman, however, in his epic poem "The Dream of Gerontius," presents us with an imaginative journey from dying to the point at which we meet God in judgment.

JOHN HENRY NEWMAN

> I suppose everyone has a great deal to say about the Providence of God over him. Every one doubtless is so watched over and tended by Him that at the last day, whether he be saved or not, he will confess that nothing could have been done for him more than had been actually done—and every one will feel his own history as special and singular.[5]

Very few of the many words penned by John Henry Newman (1801–90) have been set to music. Three compositions, however, have become universally popular in the Christian world: "Lead, Kindly Light," "Firmly I Believe and Truly," and "Praise to the Holiest in the Height." The first stands on its own. The other two are taken from Newman's epic poem "The Dream of Gerontius" (1865). These two poetic pieces, "Lead, Kindly Light" and "The Dream of Gerontius," represent the very best of Newman as a poet. I believe that the very best way into "The Dream of Gerontius" is to listen to the entirety of the Sir Edward Elgar composition with the text of "The Dream" in front of you. If this chapter leads the reader to Elgar's music, to Newman's text, and then to personal prayer, I will be well pleased.

"The Dream of Gerontius" is Newman's vision of what death (and what happens afterwards) ought to be like for a Christian. And he sees it as fundamentally hopeful. Before we look directly

5. St. John Henry Newman, in his journal for June 25, 1869, cited from Tristram, *John Henry Newman*, 268.

at Newman, let us consider other thinkers whose understanding of death is positive.

> There is a presence that walks the road of life with you. This *presence* accompanies your every moment. It shadows your every thought and feeling. On your own or with others it is always there with you. When you were born, it came out of the womb with you, with the excitement at your arrival, and nobody noticed it. Though this presence surrounds you, you may still be blind to its companionship. The name of this presence is death.[6]

These are the words of John O'Donohue, the Irish philosophical-theologian and poet. The sentiments expressed in the words initially may sound strange, but they should not be alien to the Christian. Think, for example, of St. Francis of Assisi, who speaks of death as "Sister Death." In "The Canticle of the Sun" Francis wrote, "Praised be You, my Lord, through our Sister Bodily Death." Of course, we do not always get on terribly well with our siblings. Sister Death may be one of the siblings we should like to keep at as far a distance as possible. But it isn't possible. A time will come, morning or evening, day or night, when each of us will have to die. The great insight of St. Francis is that death is "neither an enemy to be overcome nor a fate to be accepted but rather a friend, a kinsman, to be received with all courtesy."[7] We must make death a friend, strange though the language sounds. Making death a friend is of great benefit and importance. "To continually transfigure the faces of your own death ensures that at the end of your life, your physical death will be no stranger, robbing you against your will of the life that you have had; you will know its face intimately. Since you have overcome your fear, your death will be a meeting with a lifelong friend from the deepest side of your own nature."[8] This is part of what John Henry Newman was writing about in his epic poem, "The Dream of Gerontius."

6. J. O'Donohue, *Anam Chara*, 187.
7. N. O'Donoghue, *Holy Mountain*, 142.
8. J. O'Donohue, *Anam Chara*, 187.

While Newman's vision in the Dream is enormously hopeful, as we shall see, it is not a romantic vision. He realizes all too well the ambiguity that surrounds death and dying, but equally well he refuses to concede ultimacy to that ambiguity. Newman's Gerontius moves from an understandable fear to serenity and joy. That is the way it should be, especially for a Christian. Nevertheless, one can understand this fundamental ambiguity about death and dying. On the one hand, it is the end of life as we know it in this world, the severing of relationships, business left undone. One author, speaking of the Shoah and its devastation, writes, "[Those who died in the Holocaust] were torn from mistakes they had no chance to fix; everything unfinished. All the sins of love without detail, detail without love. The regret of having spoken, of having run out of time so to speak. Of hoarding oneself. Of turning one's back too often in favour of sleep."[9] On the other hand, Christians believe that death is the portal through which we go home to the Father's house, our entry point into full communion with God.

In 1864, Newman wrote his *Apologia pro Vita Sua*. The book is autobiographical in style and provides an account of Newman's growth and development in his spiritual and religious life. It was a turbulent period in Newman's life, and he seems to have had a vivid sense of his own impending death. This is the context in which "The Dream of Gerontius" was written. This sense of impending death reminds me of that fine poem written by the twentieth-century Welsh poet Dylan Thomas, "Do Not Go Gentle into That Good Night" (1951). Thomas here seems to consider the inevitability of death as something to be resisted with all one's might

It seems that the poem was written by Thomas for his dying father.[10] He watched his father grow weak and very frail with old age. Essentially he is saying to his father, Do not let your passion for life be compromised. The line "Do not go gentle into that good night" occurs four times in this short poem, and "Rage, rage against the dying of the light" occurs three times. Whether Dylan Thomas was really speaking about his father, or about himself and his own

9. Michaels, *Fugitive Pieces*, 147.

10. Gilbert, *Inventions of Farewell*, 47.

fear of death, as some critics have it, is not especially relevant for our purposes. What is relevant is the fear, and the raging against what seems to be the dying of the light of life. It is a combination of rage or anger and fear in the face of dying and death. Newman's "Gerontius" is a far cry from Dylan Thomas's advice, "Do not go gentle into that dark night." It breathes a different air.

"The Dream of Gerontius" was written over a period of three brief weeks. It was published in the periodical *The Month* in May and June 1865. Newman's method was to labor over his prose, revising and revising and revising. This text, however, seems to have sprung from deep in his soul having taken root there over the years. A friend of Newman's, Thomas William Allies, had attended an acted performance of "The Dream" in Liverpool, at a teacher-training college, and he wrote to tell Newman about it. This is how Newman describes the writing of "The Dream" by way of reply to Mr. Allies: "On the 17th of January last it came into my head to write it. I cannot really tell how, and I wrote on till it was finished, on small bits of paper."

It describes the time, if time is indeed the right word, between dying and coming before God in judgment. It paints a picture of the ideal Christian death, with the dying man being surrounded and supported in his final agony by his friends. Newman's gift for lasting friendships is well known. However, there may be another nuance to this picture. It may be literally quite true. All around the wall near Newman's bed in the Oratory in Birmingham were pictures of his friends.

The poem is about the dying of an elderly Christian, Gerontius. The word *geron* in Greek means "an old man." The poem begins with these extraordinarily moving words:

> Jesu, Maria—I am near to death,
> And thou art calling me; I know it now.
> Not by the token of this faltering breath,
> This chill at heart, this dampness on my brow,
> Jesu, have mercy! Mary, pray for me!
> 'Tis this new feeling, never felt before,
> Be with me, Lord, in my extremity!
> That I am going, that I am no more.

Gerontius has been sick before, but this is a new feeling "never felt before." The moment of dying is described as follows:

> As though my very being had given way,
> As though I was no more a substance now,
> And could fall back on nought to be my stay . . .
> And drop from out this universal frame
> Into that shapeless, scopeless, blank abyss,
> That utter nothingness, of which I came.

Newman's description is so vivid and so intense in this passage of "The Dream" that it leads one to surmise that perhaps he had an experience, an experience of mortality, or some kind of spiritual experience, that enabled him to reach this expression in the poem. This description of emptiness is followed by the prayers of the assistants, those at his bedside, and then Gerontius makes his statement of faith:

> And I hold in veneration,
> For the love of Him alone,
> Holy Church, as His creation,
> And her teachings, as His own.
> And I take with joy whatever
> Now besets me, pain or fear,
> And with a strong will I sever
> All the ties which bind me here.

This is a powerful confession of faith, that ties together his love of God with his love of the church and her teachings. He emphasizes that he "takes with joy" whatever now he is to experience. Finally, and this is very strong language, he severs "all the ties which bind him here." It is indeed a very powerful confession of his Christian faith. Yet it does not save him from the terror of death. Gerontius goes on to say:

> For now it comes again,
> That sense of ruin, which is worse than pain,
> That masterful negation and collapse
> Of all that makes me man.

His very existence, his humanity is collapsing, is being negated, as it were, by his dying and death. He is, in his own words, "falling through the solid framework of created things." Once again, the assistants pray for Gerontius, he commends himself into the hands of God, just like Jesus in St. Luke's Gospel—"into thy hands I commend my spirit"—and the priest prays that wonderful prayer for the dying: "Go forth upon thy journey, Christian soul! Go from this world! Go, in the name of God." Hearing this confident prayer, Gerontius dies. Immediately the text continues as follows:

> I went to sleep; and now I am refreshed.
> A strange refreshment: for I feel in me
> An inexpressive lightness, and a sense
> Of freedom, as I were at length myself,
> And ne'er had been before. How still it is!
> The soul of Gerontius leaves this world, and is aware of leaving this world:
> So much I know, not knowing how I know,
> That the vast universe, where I have dwelt,
> Is quitting me, or I am quitting it.

At this point, the soul feels companionship. He is not alone. His guardian angel is helping him move forward, and has come to take his soul home to the house of God.

> Someone has me fast
> Within his ample palm.

The soul of Gerontius speaks to his guardian angel:

> Why have I now no fear at meeting [God]?
> Along my earthly life, the thought of death
> And judgment was to me most terrible . . .
> Now that the hour is come, my fear is fled . . .
> Now close upon me, I can forward look
> With a serenest joy.

At this point the demons come into play, demons described as having "an animal vulgarity" as they jeer at the passing of Gerontius. Whatever one makes of these demons, it may at least be claimed that they stand for the final residue of fear, doubt, and ambiguity in the face of death.

As his natural fear of dying and death is left behind, his guardian angel carries him forward towards God, and his experience is one of joy. There is no fear. Gerontius now hears "The First Choir of the Evangelicals" singing that marvelous hymn:

> Praise to the Holiest in the height,
> And in the depth be praise:
> In all His words most wonderful;
> Most sure in all His ways!

Gerontius now enters the house of judgment. The judgment, however, comes from one whose best name is Love. There is no room for fear. Once again he hears the hymn from "The Second Choir of Evangelicals," and "The Third Choir of Evangelicals," "Praise to the Holiest in the height." His guardian angel explains to him that these evangelical choirs "sing of thy approaching agony." What agony is being spoken of here? It is the agony of seeing the God who is Love with a simultaneous recognition that one is so unlovely.

> What then—if such thy lot—thou seest thy Judge . . .
> Thou wilt be sick with love, and yearn for him . . .
> There is a pleading in his pensive eyes
> Will pierce thee to the quick, and trouble thee.
> And thou wilt hate and loathe thyself; for though
> Now sinless, thou wilt feel that thou hast sinn'd
> As never thou didst feel; and wilt desire
> To slink away, and hide thee from his sight . . .
> The shame of self at thought of seeing Him,—
> Will be thy veriest, sharpest purgatory.

These words immediately bring to my mind the eucharistic words of the priest-poet George Herbert:

> Love bade me welcome
> Yet my soul drew back guilty of dust and sin.

I am unclear whether Newman was aware of this poem, though given its popularity in his day, it seems likely. Whether he was or not, the sentiments are identical. The pain of purgatory is not some external pain inflicted upon the soul. The pain of purgatory is the recognition in the presence of Love that one is not lovely. The pain of purgatory is the intense pain of regret that one has not lived a life of love.

The intensity of purgatorial regret is expressed by Newman through Gerontius in the following words spoken by the soul to his guardian angel:

> Take me away, and in the lowest deep
> There let me be,
> And there in hope the lone night-watches keep . . .

The soul desires to move away out of a most profound sense of utter unworthiness from the presence of the God who is Love. "Take me away . . . let me be." The guardian angel who has accompanied Gerontius thus far recognizes the importance of this cleansing moment, this most intense moment of deepest regret. Gerontius feels his sinfulness. It is an immediate feeling upon coming into God's loving presence. The soul is learning that

> The flame of Everlasting Love
> Doth burn ere it transform.

"Purgatory," as Paul McPartlan rightly has it, "is the state of grace where the process of *Christification* can be perfected."[11] It is heaven's door, not hell's threshold. Nonetheless, it takes time, as it were, to be cleansed. The angel says to the soul,

> Softly and gently, dearest, sweetest soul,
> In my most loving arms I now enfold thee,
> And, o'er the penal waters, as they roll,
> I poise thee, and I lower thee, and hold thee.
> And carefully I dip thee in the lake . . .
> Farewell, but not forever! brother dear,
> Be brave and patient on thy bed of sorrow;
> Swiftly shall pass thy night of trial here,
> And I will come and wake thee on the morrow.

11. McPartlan, "Go Forth, Christian Soul," 248.

The guardian angel also tells the soul that it will be nursed and tended by angels during this purgatorial moment. It will not be left alone. Purgatory is described in this section of "The Dream" almost like a mystical state. What is the time that it takes for this cleansing to occur? "Time" seems a strange word to use now that time is over for the soul who has left this life. This time of cleansing is best understood as instantaneous. Coming before the God who is nothing but unconditional Love, one comes to understand that one has been anything but unconditional love in the living of one's life. That is the "moment" of cleansing pain, the pain of regret, the searing pain of recognizing that one cannot return to the pilgrimage on earth to undo what one ought not to have done. Nothing could hurt more, but the hurt is the consequence of the final realization that God is Love. The passage also sounds like the words in the Rite of Baptism—the soul is dipped into the lake of baptism, as it were, before being finalized as body of Christ, in God.

Newman lived through the First Vatican Council (1869–70), but the Second Vatican Council (1962–65) has been called Newman's Council. The revised liturgical rites of the church that flowed from that Council have, for the most part, been well received by the faithful throughout the world. If we leaf through the Rites for the Commendation of the Dying, we find a horizon of understanding that is truly Catholic, and so truly Newman's, as it were. In writing "The Dream" Newman reworked an ancient Latin prayer, the *Profiscere*, the first words of which are "Go forth, Christian soul." The new rite includes a formulation of this prayer. But before we get to it, we need to acknowledge the beginning of the rite. The rite says this: "One or more of the following short texts may be recited with the dying person. If necessary, they may be softly repeated two or three times." Here are some of those short scriptural texts:

> "Who can separate us from the love of Christ?" (Rom 8:35)
>
> "Whether we live or die, we are the Lord's." (Rom 14:8)
>
> "We have an everlasting home in heaven." (2 Cor 5:1)
>
> "We shall be with the Lord forever." (1 Thess 4:17)

"We shall see God as he really is." (1 John 3:2)

"Though I walk in the shadow of death, I will fear no evil,
for you are with me." (Ps 23:4)

The rite continues with further readings from Scripture and moves into the Litany of the Saints, recalling Gerontius's prayer at the beginning of the Dream: "Jesu, Maria—I am near to death . . . Jesu, have mercy! Mary, pray for me!" Then come the quite magnificent words of the Prayer of Commendation, words used "at the very cusp of the divide between life and death":

Go forth, Christian soul, from this world
In the name of God the Almighty Father,
Who created you,
In the name of Jesus Christ, Son of the living God,
Who suffered for you,
In the name of the Holy Spirit,
Who was poured out upon you,
Go forth, faithful Christian.
May you live in peace this day,
May your home be with God in Zion,
With Mary, the Virgin Mother of God,
With Joseph, and all the angels and saints.

This prayer, "Go forth, Christian soul" is the gentle nudging that may be needed to move forward from this world and to sail into the presence of God.

After death has occurred, the ritual offers various prayers among which the following may be found:

Saints of God, come to his/her aid!
Come to meet him/her, angels of the Lord!
Receive his/her soul and present him/her to God the Most High.
May Christ who called you, take you to himself;
May angels lead you to Abraham's side.

These beautiful prayers are essentially the same prayers that are reflected in "The Dream" by Newman. They indicate to us all too clearly that while there is an understandable element of fear in the unknown reality of death and dying, fear is not the *final* thing. Rather, it is a quiet hopeful confidence of coming into God's lovely presence. This is the meaning of Newman's "Dream of Gerontius."

Why not just read the text? Why listen to the musical composition of Sir Edward Elgar? Does the music add anything to this text? I am no musician. But Newman himself said, "I always sleep better after music. . . . Perhaps thought is music."

However, I find these words of a theologian reflecting on what music does to us particularly persuasive:

> To listen seriously to music and to perform it are among our most potent ways of learning what it is to live with and before God. . . . In this "obedience" of listening and following, we are stretched and deepened, physically challenged as performers, imaginatively as listeners. The time we have renounced, given up, is given back to us as a time in which we have become more human, more real, even (or especially) when we can't say what we have learned, only that we have changed.[12]

The claim is being made that listening seriously to music changes us. We are made different by the music. We are stretched and deepened. We are made more human. Too few things in life stretch and deepen us. Music has the capacity to do this. Being aware of the text, and listening to Elgar's composition of "The Dream of Gerontius" seems to me a uniquely privileged moment of grace. Grace is God reaching out to us, in this case reaching out through word and music. We are changed.

Sir Edward Elgar composed the oratorio "The Dream of Gerontius" in 1900. It was composed for the Birmingham Music Festival and its first performance took place in Birmingham Town Hall on October 3, 1900. Birmingham then, as now, is a very ordinary city, an industrial center, a city of ordinary working people. There is something entirely appropriate about the first performance of "The Dream of Gerontius" taking place in Birmingham. Birmingham Town Hall is about three miles from the Birmingham Oratory

12. Williams, *Open to Judgment*, 248.

on the Hagley Road, founded by Newman, and in which he composed "The Dream." Birmingham was a far cry from the elegance of Oxford and its university. Yet it was in Birmingham that Blessed John Henry Newman lived, prayed and worshiped, ministered to the people, and died. It was in the industrial city of Birmingham that John Henry Newman opened a church in what had been previously a gin distillery. He cared for the very ordinary people of Birmingham. When invited by the rather pompous Monsignor George Talbot to preach a series of Lenten sermons to his genteel English congregation in Rome, advising Newman that he "would have a more educated Audience of Protestants than could ever be the case in England," Newman replied curtly, "Birmingham people have souls, and I have neither taste nor talent for the sort of work which you cut out for me: and I beg to decline your offer."[13] It was one of the best literary snubs in English. Arguably it was for the ordinary Christian folk that "The Dream of Gerontius" had been written. Ordinary folk can still benefit in great measure from it.

A FEW WORDS FROM KALLISTOS WARE

Leaving poetry behind we turn now to the theologian Kallistos Ware (1934–2022), formerly known as Timothy Ware. Kallistos Ware was a gifted Orthodox theologian and his many publications helped and continue to help to make the world of theology more aware of the Eastern Orthodox tradition. In 2023 a volume of Ware's theology, *Sacraments of Healing*, was posthumously published.[14] Ware's style and expression are so pleasing. Reaching into the rich tradition of Orthodox theology and reflection, and sharing illuminating examples from his own experience, he provides us with a very hope-filled vision of death. The chapter in his book is entitled "'A Peaceful Ending to Our Life', Bodily Death as an Experience of Healing." It is full of Christian wisdom.

13. See the exchange in Ward, *Life of John Henry Cardinal Newman*, 2:539.

14. I am most grateful to my colleague at Mount Angel Seminary, Dr. Anna Petrin, for drawing my attention to this text.

Close to the beginning of the chapter Ware quotes from St. Isaac the Syrian:

> Fix your departure in your heart, O man, by always saying to yourself: "Behold, the messenger is at the door, he who comes for me. Why am I idle? My going forth is forever; there will be no return." Pass the night in this reflection; muse upon this thought throughout the day. And when the time of departure comes, meet it with gladness, saying: "Come in peace! I knew that you were coming, and I have not neglected anything that could prove useful to me on the way."[15]

The passage brings to mind some of the sentiments of Emily Dickinson above. Death is seen not as an enemy to be avoided, and, in Ware's words, the passage is permeated by a "gentle realism and a sense of peacefulness."

Having set the tone of the chapter with St. Isaac the Syrian, Ware goes on to provide some realistic counsel about preparation for death. The first thing he notes is the preparation of a will. This reduces greatly the burden of things to be attended to by others once one has died. Next, comes something far more important: mutual forgiveness. Ware writes, "We should seek to be reconciled with all those from whom we are estranged. We should ask pardon and accept it, and we should take care not to leave this for the last moment, for we do not know when the last moment will come."[16] Needless to say, this is far from easy, but it is common sense and solid spiritual advice!

Ware now proceeds two aspects of death. The first is how death and birth go together. "Before our great death, the end of our life, we pass through many other deaths, and in each stage in our life death goes with growth. So perhaps we should see death as the final stage in our growth as persons."[17] This is a way of understand-

15. Isaac the Syrian, Homily 64, in his *Ascetical Homilies*, 459, cited in Ware, *Sacraments of Healing*, 93.

16. Ware, *Sacraments of Healing*, 94.

17. Ware, *Sacraments of Healing*, 95.

ing death echoed by many other spiritual authors. In a sense it is our final human experience of the Paschal Mystery, out of death life, the rhythm of the universe, as it were. It is fundamentally the recognition that in Ware's words, "The whole of life is a constant passover, passing over through death into new life. We should never think of death alone; we should always think of death and resurrection."[18] Approaching death as a sacrament of healing leading into final communion with God requires constant practice if it is to be effective. If keeping death before our eyes in this healing fashion becomes part and parcel of our daily practice, we shall be as prepared as possible for its advent in our lives.

CONCLUSION

This little book grew out of a lifelong interest in "evil, suffering, and thinking about God." In graduate school the issue was tackled for the most part in courses on the philosophy of religion. As I come closer to the end of my theological pilgrimage the focus has changed. Evil and suffering remain challenging for a Christian, as indeed for everyone. Now, however, instead of seeing theodicy in primarily problematic terms, I have been led to think about it in terms of the triune God and the incarnate Christ.

How does one conclude this series of snapshots on the challenges posed for Christians by the experience of evil and suffering in life? Continuing to think critically seems to me both natural and, indeed, essential. We are intelligent beings. However, continuing to love God and to be drawn into ever deeper communion with him, in Christ, through the Spirit, is more important. This demands cultivating the mystical-cosmic-corporate vision of the cross throughout life—regular personal prayer, regular participation in the sacraments, regular reading of the Scriptures, and regular reaching out in kindness to others by becoming beacons of hope and sacraments of love. A lifetime's task.

18. Ware, *Sacraments of Healing*, 96–97.

Bibliography

Allchin, A. M. *The World Is a Wedding*. New York: Oxford University Press, 1968.

Andreopoulos, Andreas. *The Sign of the Cross: The Gesture, the Mystery, the History*. Brewster, MA: Paraclete, 2006.

Arendt, Hannah. *Eichmann in Jerusalem: A Report on the Banality of Evil*. Rev. ed. New York: Penguin, 1965.

Augustine. "Exposition of Psalm 62, 2." In *The Works of St. Augustine: A Translation for the 21st Century, Expositions of the Psalms, III/18*. Hyde Park, NY: New City, 2002.

———. "Exposition of Psalm 85, 1." In *The Works of St. Augustine: A Translation for the 21st Century, Expositions of the Psalms, III/18*. Hyde Park, NY: New City, 2002.

Barron, Robert. "God." In *The Blackwell Companion to Catholicism*, edited by James J. Buckley et al, 268–81. Oxford: Blackwell, 2007.

Beattie, Tina. *The Good Priest*. Leicester, UK: Troubadour, 2019.

Benedict of Canfield. *The Holy Will of God: A Short Rule of Perfection*. Translated by Fr. Collins. London: Thomas Richardson, 1878.

Brown, Andrew. Obituary of Margaret Spufford. *The Guardian*, Mar. 20, 2014.

Bulgakov, Sergius. *The Eucharistic Sacrifice*. Notre Dame: University of Notre Dame Press, 2021.

Burtchaell, James T. *Philemon's Problem*. Grand Rapids: Eerdmans, 2001.

Catechism of the Catholic Church. Washington, DC: United States Catholic Conference of Bishops, 1995.

Collins, John J. *Introduction to the Hebrew Bible*. 2nd ed. Minneapolis: Fortress, 2014.

Cottingham, John. *The Spiritual Dimension: Religion, Philosophy and Human Value*. Cambridge: Cambridge University Press, 2005.

Crews, Rowan. *Good Lord, Deliver Us: The Praise of God and the Problem of Evil*. Akron, OH: OSL, 2001.

Cummings, Owen F. *How Great Thou Art: Theological Perspectives on Creation*. Eugene, OR: Cascade, 2024.

———. *John Macquarrie: A Master of Theology*. Mahwah, NJ: Paulist, 2002.

———. *Miracles in the Christian Tradition*. Mahwah, NJ: Paulist, 2021.

———. *Popes, Councils, and Theology*. Eugene, OR: Pickwick, 2021.

———. *Thinking About Prayer*. Eugene, OR: Wipf and Stock, 2009.

Daly, Gabriel. *Asking the Father*. Dublin: Dominican, 1982.

Davidson, Robert. *The Courage to Doubt: Exploring an Old Testament Theme*. London: SCM, 1983.

Davis, Ellen F. *Opening Israel's Scriptures*. New York: Oxford University Press, 2019.

Dawkins, Richard. *The God Delusion*. London: Bantam, 2006.

Duffy, Eamon. *Walking to Emmaus*. New York: Burns and Oates, 2006.

Duffy, Stephen J. "Evil." In *The New Dictionary of Catholic Spirituality*, edited by Michael Downey, 361–64. Collegeville, MN: Liturgical, 1993.

Eagleton, Terry. "Lunging, Flailing, Mispunching." *London Review of Books* 28 (Oct. 19, 2006). https://www.lrb.co.uk/the-paper/v28/n20/terry-eagleton/lunging-flailing-mispunching.

Eaton, John H. *The Psalms*. New York: Continuum, 2005.

Ford, David F. *The Shape of Living*. London: Collins, 1997.

———. *Theology: A Very Short Introduction*. Oxford: Oxford University Press, 1999.

Dickinson, Emily. *The Poems of Emily Dickinson*. Edited by R. W. Franklin. Cambridge, MA: Belknap, 1999.

Gallagher, Michael Paul. *The Human Poetry of Faith*. Mahwah, NJ: Paulist, 2003.

Gigliotti, Marcus A. "Portrait of an Artist in Pain." In *The Bible on Suffering: Social and Political Implications*, edited by Anthony J. Tambasco, 72–92. Mahwah, NJ: Paulist, 2001.

Gilbert, Sandra M., ed. *Inventions of Farewell: A Book of Elegies*. New York: Norton, 2001.

Greene, Graham. *The Heart of the Matter*. Harmondsworth, UK: Penguin, 1999.

Greene-McCreight, Kathryn. *Darkness Is My Only Companion: A Christian Response to Mental Illness*. Grand Rapids: Brazos, 2006.

Grove, Kevin G. *Augustine on Memory*. Oxford: Oxford University Press, 2021.

Gutiérrez, Gustavo. *On Job*. Maryknoll, NY: Orbis, 1996.

Halik, Tomas. *Night of the Confessor*. New York: Image, 2012.

Hardy, Daniel W., and David F. Ford. *Jubilate: Theology in Praise*. London: Darton, Longman and Todd, 1984.

Hardy, Daniel W., et al. *Wording a Radiance: Parting Conversations on God and the Church*. London: SCM, 2010.

Harrington, Daniel. *Why Do We Suffer?* Lanham, MD: Sheed and Ward, 2000.

Hayes, Zachary. *The Gift of Being: A Theology of Creation*. Collegeville, MN: Liturgical, 2001.

Hays, Richard B. "The Story of God's Son: The Identity of Jesus in the Letters of Paul." In *Seeking the Identity of Jesus*, edited by Beverly Roberts Gaventa and Richard B. Hays, 180–99. Grand Rapids: Eerdmans, 2008.

Hick, John. *Evil and the God of Love*. New York: Harper and Row, 1978.

Hooker, Morna D., and Frances M. Young. *Holiness and Mission*. London: SCM, 2010.

Hosinski, Thomas E. *The Image of the Unseen God: Catholicity, Science and Our Evolving Understanding of God*. Maryknoll, NY: Orbis, 2017.

Houston, Joseph. *Reported Miracles*. Cambridge: Cambridge University Press, 1994.

Hügel, Friedrich von. *The Mystical Element of Religion*. 1909. Reprint, Rome: Aeterna, 2015.

Isaac the Syrian. *Ascetical Homilies*. Brookline, MA: Holy Transfiguration Monastery, 2011.

Jasper, David. "Echoes of Laughter: Why Theologians Should Read Novels." *Theology* 106 (2003) 414.

Kilby, Karen. *God, Evil and the Limits of Theology*. London: T&T Clark, 2020.

Kilby, Karen, and Rachel Davies, eds. *Suffering and the Christian Life*. London: T&T Clark, 2020.

Kushner, Harold. *When Bad Things Happen to Good People*. New York: Avon, 1981.

Lane, Dermot A. *Keeping Hope Alive*. Mahwah, NJ: Paulist, 1996.

Lash, Nicholas. "On Learning to Be Wise." *Priests and People* 15 (2001) 355–59.

———. *Theology for Pilgrims*. London: Darton, Longman and Todd, 2008.

Lewis, C. S. *A Grief Observed*. New York: Bantam, 1963.

———. *The Problem of Pain*. London: Collins, 1949.

MacKenzie, R. A. F., and R. E. Murphy. "Job." In *The New Jerome Biblical Commentary*, edited by R. E. Brown et al. Englewood Cliffs, NJ: Prentice-Hall, 1990.

Macquarrie, John. *Principles of Christian Theology*. Rev. ed. London: SCM, 1977.

Martin, George. "Psalm 44: Suffering 'for the Sake of' God." In *The Bible on Suffering*, edited by Anthony J. Tambasco, 18–33. Mahwah, NJ: Paulist, 2001.

McCabe, Herbert. *God Matters*. London: Chapman, 1987.

———. *God Still Matters*. New York: Continuum, 2002.

McKenzie, John L. *Dictionary of the Bible*. Milwaukee: Bruce, 1965.

McPartlan, Paul. "Go Forth, Christian Soul." *One in Christ* 34 (1998) 247–57.

Merton, Thomas. *Elected Silence*. London: Hollis & Carter, 1949.

Michaels, Anne. *Fugitive Pieces*. London: Bloomsbury, 1998.

Moule, C. F. D. *The Origin of Christology*. Cambridge: Cambridge University Press, 1977.

Murphy, Roland E. *The Tree of Life: An Exploration of Wisdom Literature*. 2nd ed. Grand Rapids: Eerdmans, 1996.

Murray, Paul D. "Living Sacrifice: Is There a Non-Pathological Way of Living Sacrifice?" In *Suffering and the Christian Life*, edited by Karen Kilby and Rachel Davies, 189–206. London: T&T Clark, 2020.

Norris, Kathleen. *Acedia and Me*. New York: Riverhead, 2008.

Nowell, Irene. *Pleading, Cursing, Praising*. Collegeville, MN: Liturgical, 2013.

O'Donoghue, Noel Dermot, ODC. *The Holy Mountain: Approaches to the Mystery of Prayer*. Wilmington, DE: Glazier, 1983.

O'Donohue, John. *Anam Chara*. New York: HarperCollins, 1997.

Owen, Huw Parri. *Concepts of Deity*. New York: Herder and Herder, 1971.

Radcliffe, Timothy, OP. *Take the Plunge*. London: Bloomsbury, 2012.

Rahner, Karl. "Saying Yes to God with Hope and Love." *The Universe*, Lent 1984.

Raschko, Michael B. *A Christian Understanding of Human Nature*. New London, CT: Twenty-Third, 2010.

Ratzinger, Joseph. *"In the beginning . . .": A Catholic Understanding of the Story of Creation and the Fall*. Grand Rapids: Eerdmans, 1995.

Ryan, Robin. *God and the Mystery of Human Suffering*. Mahwah, NJ: Paulist, 2011.

———. *Life Is Changed, Not Ended*. Mahwah, NJ: Paulist, 2024.

Sheldrake, Philip. *Love Took My Hand: The Spirituality of George Herbert*. Cambridge, MA: Cowley, 2000.

Simon, Ulrich. *Theology of Auschwitz*. London: Gollancz, 1967.

Soskice, Janet M. "Why *Creatio ex Nihilo* for Theology Today?" In *Creation ex Nihilo: Origins, Development, Contemporary Challenges*, edited by Gary A. Anderson and Markus Bockmuehl, 37–54. Notre Dame: University of Notre Dame Press, 2018.

Sparks, Richard. "Suffering." In *The New Dictionary of Catholic Spirituality*, edited by Michael Downey, 950–53. Collegeville, MN: Liturgical, 1993.

Spufford, Margaret. *Celebration: A Story of Suffering and Joy*. London: Mowbray, 1989.

Styron, William. *Sophie's Choice*. London: Corgi, 1979.

Surin, Kenneth. "Atonement and Moral Apocalypticism: William Styron's *Sophie's Choice*." Chapter 7 in *The Turnings of Darkness and Light: Essays in Philosophical and Systematic Theology*. Cambridge: Cambridge University Press, 1989.

———. *Theology and the Problem of Evil*. 1986. Reprint, Eugene, OR: Wipf and Stock, 2004.

Sykes, Stephen. *Unashamed Anglicanism*. Nashville: Abingdon, 1995.

Terrien, Samuel. *The Psalms*. Grand Rapids: Eerdmans, 2003.

Tilley, Terrence W. "Evil, Problem of." In *The New Dictionary of Theology*, edited by Joseph A. Komonchak et al., 360–63. Collegeville, MN: Liturgical, 1987.

———. *Evils of Theodicy*. 1991. Reprint, Eugene, OR: Wipf and Stock, 2000.

Tristram, Henry, ed. *John Henry Newman: Autobiographical Writings*. New York: Sheed and Ward, 1957.

Van Bavel, Tarcisius. "The Meaninglessness of Suffering." In *God and Human Suffering*, edited by Jan Lambrecht and Raymond F. Collins, 121–36. Louvain: Peeters, 1990.

———. "Where Is God When Human Beings Suffer?" In *God and Human Suffering*, edited by Jan Lambrecht and Raymond F. Collins, 137–53. Louvain: Peeters, 1990.

Vann, Gerald. *The Pain of Christ and the Sorrow of God*. 1947. Reprint, Manchester, NH: Sophia Institute, 2020.

Ward, Wilfrid. *The Life of John Henry Cardinal Newman: Based on His Private Journals and Correspondence*. London: Longmans, Green, and Co., 1912. https://www.newmanreader.org/biography/ward/index.html.

Walsh, James, and P. G. Walsh. *Divine Providence and Human Suffering*. Wilmington, DE: Glazier, 1985.

Ware, Kallistos. *Sacraments of Healing*. Yonkers, NY: St. Vladimir's Seminary Press, 2023.

Weil, Simone. *Waiting for God*. New York: Putnam's Sons, 1951.

Weiser, Artur. *The Psalms, A Commentary*. London: SCM, 1962.

Williams, Rowan D. *Christ the Heart of Creation*. London: Bloomsbury, 2018.

———. *Open to Judgment: Sermons and Addresses*. London: Darton, Longman and Todd, 1994.

———. *Tokens of Trust*. Louisville: Westminster John Knox, 2007.

Wright, John H. "God." In *The New Dictionary of Theology*, edited by J. A. Komonchak et al., 423–36. Collegeville, MN: Liturgical, 1987.

Yarnold, Edward. *The Theology of Original Sin*. Cork: Mercier, 1971.

Young, Frances M. *Brokenness and Blessing*. London: Darton, Longman and Todd, 2007.

———. *Face to Face: A Narrative Essay in the Theology of Suffering*. Edinburgh: T&T Clark, 1990.

———. "Suffering." In *The Oxford Companion to Christian Thought*, edited by Adrian Hastings et al., 687–89. Oxford: Oxford University Press, 2000.

www.ingramcontent.com/pod-product-compliance
Lightning Source LLC
LaVergne TN
LVHW090527110826
845146LV00003B/1008

* 9 7 9 8 3 8 5 2 6 2 6 7 0 *